CRACK the **CUSTOMER MIND** CODE

Also Authored by Gary Hennerberg

Direct Marketing Quantified:
The Knowledge is in the Numbers

Urges: Hope and Inspiration for People with
Trichotillomania and Other Mysterious Disorders

CRACK the CUSTOMER MIND CODE

SEVEN PATHWAYS FROM
HEAD -> HEART -> YES!

GARY HENNERBERG

New York

CRACK the CUSTOMER MIND CODE
Seven Pathways from Head -> Heart -> Yes!

© 2016 **GARY HENNERBERG**.

Published in New York, New York, by Morgan James Publishing. Morgan James and The Entrepreneurial Publisher are trademarks of Morgan James, LLC.
www.MorganJamesPublishing.com

The Morgan James Speakers Group can bring authors to your live event. For more information or to book an event visit The Morgan James Speakers Group at www.TheMorganJamesSpeakersGroup.com.

Shelfie

A **free** eBook edition is available
with the purchase of this print book.

CLEARLY PRINT YOUR NAME ABOVE IN UPPER CASE

Instructions to claim your free eBook edition:
1. Download the Shelfie app for Android or iOS
2. Write your name in **UPPER CASE** above
3. Use the Shelfie app to submit a photo
4. Download your eBook to any device

ISBN 978-1-63047-698-4 paperback
ISBN 978-1-63047-699-1 eBook
Library of Congress Control Number:
2015911257

Cover Design by:
John Weber

Interior Design by:
Bonnie Bushman
The Whole Caboodle Graphic Design

In an effort to support local communities and raise awareness and funds, Morgan James Publishing donates a percentage of all book sales for the life of each book to Habitat for Humanity Peninsula and Greater Williamsburg.

Get involved today, visit
www.MorganJamesBuilds.com

Habitat
for Humanity®
Peninsula and
Greater Williamsburg
Building Partner

"These seven pathways aren't just a theory. The process is proven. And it works."

TABLE OF CONTENTS

ACKNOWLEDGEMENTS

Crack the Customer Mind Code weaves a deeply personal story about the inner-workings of my mind along with my life's work as a marketing consultant and copywriter.

As a child, little did I know that my own mind mystery and curiosity would ultimately become a strength with good coming from it. In the pages ahead, you'll read the story of my struggle with a compulsive disorder that profoundly impacted my childhood, teen years, and even my early adult years.

Before jumping into my story, there are several people who deserve to be acknowledged:

- My wife LoCinda, for being my soulmate who has enabled so many lifetime opportunities. She has given me the encouragement and support to pursue my dreams.
- My parents, who have been a huge blessing in my life. When I was a child, they were the best parents a child with a mysterious obsessive-compulsive disorder could have had to encourage me to discover my gifts and talents.
- My daughters Amy and Liza, for becoming fine young women who I can proudly say have applied marketing knowledge in their careers. The apple hasn't fallen far from the tree.
- My colleague since 1996, Perry Alexander, who encourages me to pause and reflect, then challenge my ideas. Our back-and-forth discussions have resulted in stronger whole-brain thinking.
- The staff at Morgan James Publishing who have taken a dream and helped me put it in the tangible form that you are holding in your

hands. And the many authors and author support people I've come to know from Author101 University.

- My editors at North American Publishing and *Target Marketing Magazine* who published my first article in 1993 and have now published hundreds of my articles, blog posts, videos and webinars for more than two decades.

- My friends at American Writers and Artists who for over a decade have invited me to speak at events on numerous occasions and teach aspiring copywriters. I've learned much from you and my students.

- And finally, my singing brothers in Vocal Majority who know how to make an audience of raving fans *feel* good. There are hundreds of passionate men who I've come to know in Vocal Majority since I first auditioned and became a chorus performer in 1993. Two of whom deserve special recognition are the directors, motivators and my friends, father-son duo Jim Clancy and Greg Clancy. You have taught me how to sing from the heart and to never be afraid to express emotion. I can't imagine life without Vocal Majority and the privilege to perform for, inspire, and touch the lives and emotions of thousands of people year-after-year. Much more will be revealed in the pages ahead about Vocal Majority and the cross-media marketing campaigns I've created for this internationally-renowned chorus.

Please come along now for a fascinating journey with the natural flow of pathways through the human mind.

INTRODUCTION

As a child, I was consumed with a mysterious obsessive-compulsive disorder. I pulled my hair. That compulsion has woven a complex fabric of memories and curiosities in my mind. For years I felt like I was alone, and that I was the only person on the planet with this bizarre urge to pull my hair. I repeatedly asked myself, "why me?"

This compulsion is still a part of my life, and it's hard-coded in my mind. And it's this compulsion that forms the basis of my curiosity about the mind and emotions.

Since my childhood, I've sought to understand my own mind and what compels me to take the actions that I do in my life. I've concluded that I'm not alone in having profound emotional feelings and deeply engrained memory grooves in my mind. I'm convinced most of us have an "issue" of some kind that forms deep grooves in the mind, and that at some level most people seek affirmations to satisfy individual emotional needs or "issues."

My obsession is to understand deeper thinking, and the pathways in the mind that motivate people to take action. The concepts I'll share in this book may well upend how you approach marketing, advertising and selling. They can influence how you can powerfully interact with people around you, how you can more successfully work with, or manage, people in an organization, and how you can transform your personal life by understanding the memory grooves in the mind and how you can use those pathways to your advantage.

You are the person you are today as a result of accumulated lifetime experiences. That accumulation of experience weaves a complex fabric of memories that influences how you think and how your mind is stimulated, calmed, and makes decisions. And people seek out affirmation of those decisions.

Applying these principles to marketing, creating new memories and altering existing memory often requires retraining both your current and prospective customers' and donors' mind code. Your repeated thoughts carve grooves in the pathways of your consciousness, and soon a thought process goes, for illustration purposes, from a dirt path to a gravel lane … from gravel to a 2-lane road … to a 4-lane highway … and to a high-speed super highway.

Simply stated: you can instill new memory by taking your prospective customer or donor through a sequence of mind pathways proven to create new memory grooves.

Creating new memory requires re-patterning or re-coding the neuropathways. Think of neuropathways as corridors or pathways in the brain—thought patterns, automatic reactions, and importantly, ingrained habits. It's what enables us to know how to walk or drive without consciously thinking about it. Or if you're like most people, when you get up in the morning, you have a routine that seldom deviates. When you change your routine, you probably find yourself wondering if you have forgotten something. Or you try to fill in what you were thinking before your mind when blank. So you go back and check, and perhaps recheck until you have resolved in your mind that you're back on the right track. Once you establish a habit, your subconscious mind automatically does things for you. This is because you have created a neuropathway in your brain. A groove.

But there is a formulation of the mind that predates grooving memories. When you were born, your mind was already wired for the living and breathing species that you are as a human.

As you develop and mature, you begin to react and process information and messages with a blend of emotions and logic. Deep down, how your brain reacts to stimuli, and the hormones and chemicals that are released in the brain shape how you react and respond to the world around you.

Even though culture and technology change and evolve, your mind is still primitive. It's easy to think your mind has changed over the generations, but that's not really the case. You have an emotional control panel that filters and processes stimuli. The reality in this "always-on" mobile world is that marketers have to approach messaging using a flow that naturally conforms to memory grooves in the mind. The opportunity you have is to influence how your prospects respond with the primitive mind using proven approaches, but with the twist of using today's multi-channel media world.

MUSIC NEVER ENDS

A metaphor that uses music may serve to bring clarity to the sequences of how the mind paves a new pathway. Music is generally accepted as contributing to a person's memory. Even if you're not a participant in vocal or instrumental music, you've heard jingles on radio and television that help you recall a brand or business name. For example, if you're over around the age of 40, when you read the words, "I'd like to teach the world to sing" you might also "hear" those words set to music, and you instantly associate it with Coke.

So thinking like a performing musician, there is a process of how a memory is deeply grooved to enable learning a new song and most importantly, to present it powerfully for an audience.

My social media followers and blog readers are aware that I'm a performer with an internationally-acclaimed and award-winning men's chorus based in Dallas, Texas. All 100-plus members are volunteers in Vocal Majority (VocalMajority. com) and we love to sing. We're good. Damned good. The key to our success is that we move audience emotions in ways and places that continue to put me in awe. The chorus is so good that the chorus has won (as of this writing) 12 International Gold Medal Championships from the Barbershop Harmony Society. I first joined the organization in 1993, and for many years have handled marketing for the chorus.

Every week's rehearsal is a combination of motivation, positive emotion reinforcement, and creating memory for notes, words, and choreography. Over the years, I've come to appreciate how this weekly ritual has made me a better husband, father, business consultant and human being.

So as I have searched for a metaphor to establish how marketers can create stronger messaging, I look no further than the process Vocal Majority performers go through to take a song from seeing "the spots" (or more formally stated, the printed music) for the first time, all the way to emotionally moving our audiences to standing ovations (which happens with regularity).

There is a process the performing chorus must go through to learn new music. Everyone struggles a bit at first. We listen to learning tracks so we can learn on our own outside of rehearsal. We sing along with the learning track at home or while driving. Over time, the notes and rhythm become more familiar. Eventually the music is memorized in the mind, but only until the music is automatic in delivery can it be genuinely sung from the heart. Watch any popular talent shows on television, such as The Voice or America's Got Talent, and just by watching a performer, you can sense if he or she is singing from the heart, or nervously singing from memory.

This process is the same when you are introducing concepts and messages about your organization or product to your prospective customers or donors. It takes time for the consumer to absorb your message.

The steps a musician takes, and how that process reinforces the premise of this book, can be explained in these seven pathways:

1. **Personality.** Before any musician delves into the music, she or he studies the personality of the score, and quickly notes if it is a ballad, or energy-filled uptune.

2. **Stimulate Emotion**. The very first notes of a song quickly reveal its emotion. A song written in a major key most often evokes happy emotions; a minor key: sad emotions.

3. **Calm the Soul.** Music is often a way for people to slow down from a hectic day, or it can be a way to energize someone who is having a "down" day. Both conditions benefit from calming. As a performer, we look for the place in the score to calm the soul, even if "calming" is actually lifting a person up.

4. **Uniqueness of the Song.** A newly written song has to breakthrough to the listener. Think back to the first time you heard a new song. Some are catchy and you want to hear them again. That song becomes a Top 40 hit. Others—the ones that are never hits—don't resonate. When you hear a new arrangement of a familiar song (often the case for Vocal Majority repertoire), there must be an interesting "positioning" or "repositioning" of the song that sets it apart from every other arrangement of the song.

5. **Storytelling.** Great vocal music doesn't have complicated notes and sounds: it is often popular because of a story told in the lyrics. A story engages. People are drawn in. The best songs tell a story, and it's the role of the performer to tell that story.

6. **Interpret.** The choral performer must interpret the song for the listener. Even though the song is delivered in sound, it's actually the visual expression on the face of the performer that cues the audience to the feel of the music.

7. **Permission to Act.** The ultimate reward for the performer is an enthusiastic reception from the audience that includes a standing ovation. How does the performer achieve it? By welling up emotional feeling. Sending chills. Raising goosebumps on the arms. The requirement to move audience to enthusiastically give themselves permission to respond: singing from the heart.

I'll circle back later to this metaphor of taking music from introduction to standing ovation and compare it to that of a marketing performance. The question to be addressed is how do you create marketing campaigns that deliver a standing ovation?

INFLUENCING THE DECISIONS PEOPLE MAKE

With the realization that the human mind is coded in specific ways, it would seem, then, that marketers can be more successful in many aspects of individual lives when messages align with the pathways that, as humans, inevitably are used to make decisions.

I've long been fascinated with how the brain is wired and why people take the actions that they do. My curiosity in this complex process is one reason I've worked in marketing as a strategist, copywriter, and analyst for my entire career.

Since the 1970s, I've created and observed advertising and sales campaigns in print and broadcast. Now, for over a decade, I've created online channel marketing campaigns. Some advertising and marketing messages that I've created have produced respectable results. Too many, I can admit after trial and error, didn't move the needle very far, and a few: not at all. It's in my more seasoned years, and after applying the process of stimulating emotion and appealing to logic flowing along the pathway of the mind, that I generate more successes than mediocre results.

It wasn't until I deeply analyzed the thought process of what worked, and what didn't, that I can conclude there are seven pathways in the head (and the heart) that can influence how people process stimuli and act. Drawing the inferences between what works for me and what I know works for other marketers, then matching those steps to the pathways in the brain, sparked an epiphany of how it all comes together.

Thankfully, I have the numbers to prove which of my marketing and sales programs have moved the sales needle significantly. In my quest to understand why certain sales and marketing campaigns have worked, I've paused, reflected and analyzed those campaigns to observe the reasons why some worked, and some didn't.

Before mapping out how I have arrived at this point, it's appropriate to pause and reflect on cultural factors that influence marketing success. You can't ignore cultural factors. They influence thinking and the response generated from prospective customers and donors.

THREE CULTURAL FACTORS

The cultural landscape is changing and evolving faster and faster with each generation, but the wiring in the brain doesn't change. While your prospect's mind grooves and memory change rapidly, their instinctive emotional reactions are timeless. Long-term memories are deeply grooved. You must create new emotional memories. The competition for attention is overwhelming. Yet, some marketers are stuck in what once worked and are afraid to leave a comfort zone built over decades of success. However, agile and smart marketers constantly reinvent and think more deeply than ever before.

What's driving this most recent rapid change? I think it's a combination from the shifting of three factors since the turn to the 21st century:

1. **Technology.** Technological change is ongoing and steady, but a huge breakthrough for practical day-to-day use comes with the introduction

of social media. Our culture embraces it and it's a part of everyday life. It began in the business-to-business category with LinkedIn and for consumers with MySpace in 2003. Facebook came online in 2004, YouTube in 2005, and Twitter in 2006. Additional spin-offs and new ventures appear often. On social media channels, users share stories daily to millions of people. Social media is a platform where positive events and situations occur every second, every day.

2. **Money.** Economic hardship culminating with the markets falling off a cliff in 2008 pose lingering negative psychological effects for years to come, just as the Great Depression in the 1930s left indelible attitudes for generations before us. The "Greatest Generation" will never forget those dark times. Those memories continue to linger with that generation. It stands to reason that any people hit hard by the Great Recession starting in 2008 will also struggle with bad memories for years to come. Negativity and darkness can be difficult to lift, and as you'll learn more about later, the human mind is wired to naturally gravitate toward negative messages.

3. **Struggle.** Political struggle, including a significant shift in national and state-level leadership with swings from one polarizing view to another, lingers on with distracting daily headlines in the media. One of the greatest negative influences is the barrage of daily news, shouting commentators, and negative political advertising. The human mind is wired for negativity, and the constant grooving of negativity from headlines and national leadership deepens already dark emotions.

Combined, over the past decade these three elements exacerbate skepticism at all levels. Financial and political negativity intensify fear, uncertainty and doubt.

These high-level, big picture cultural factors influence how people respond to your marketing messages. People are inundated with advertising and marketing messages in mass broadcast media, print, online channels, in their mailboxes and more. But today, digital technology empowers people to research you and your product or service. While scrutinizing you online, they spot your competitors.

Some marketers and clients say that they don't want an online component in their offline marketing campaigns because it will make it too easy for their prospect to research and compare. Though it may currently work for people who haven't grown up with or adapted to online technology, that segment of people is gradually aging out.

In reality, the media of choice, whether offline or online, can be made more effective when following the sequence of seven decision-making pathways of the mind. These are pathways that help individuals process your message, create new memory grooves, and go to a mental place where they give themselves permission to act. Deep human emotions in the mind—the wiring of the brain—are timeless. It's tough to create new memory grooves. But it's imperative for marketers to succeed.

Your challenge, then, is to reach deeper, and follow the mind channel sequences of the brain that influence the real human reasons that motivate response. To be successful in today's culture, marketers need to be authentic and credible. You need to understand the pathways of the mind and how to pave new memory grooves that contribute to people being motivated by your messaging and offers.

In the upcoming pages, you'll learn more about this seven-step process I see as part of the mind's decision tree. I'll also share 12 personas that I have identified and observed in more than 35 years as a marketing consultant and copywriter. These conclusions come from my experience working with marketing organizations representing dozens of product and service categories. Those categories span the business-to-consumer, business-to-business, non-profit, and agricultural sectors. You'll learn insights into what keeps your prospects, customers and donors awake at night. You'll discover how to stimulate emotion, calm the mind, position your organization and what you sell, engage with storytelling, interpret the offer, and open up the affirming permission to respond. And to illustrate these points, I'll offer suggestions of how to approach each of the 12 personas for all seven of these mind channel processes.

Most importantly, you'll understand how to use these pathways for specific types of personas, all based on my experience with messaging that has reached tens of millions of consumers, businesses, and donors around the world.

If you are curious about how the pathways of the mind work to process messaging, this should be a fascinating ride into understanding how deep grooves of memory are formed in the mind, and how you can influence and repave those grooves with new memory.

CHAPTER 1

THE MIND AND THREE IMPERATIVES

In an "always-on" culture, you and your prospects may be juggling multiple media stimuli at any one time.

Assuming you're like most people in these times, you're multitasking on your smartphone, tablet, laptop, TV, or other media device. And so are your prospects. Intuition tells us that it's tough to media multitask, that is, to simultaneously use two or more media devices. If you've done it, you know you're not completely present with any one of the devices. Rather, your focus diverts from one media to the other, resulting in missing pieces from both stimuli.

It's been proven that the brain cannot multitask. People aren't wired that way. In an awareness test experiment as reported in LiveScience[1], subjects were asked to watch a video and count how many passes occurred between basketball players wearing white shirts. Halfway through the video, a person in a gorilla suit walked across the court, but a majority of the subjects didn't notice the gorilla at all. This gave evidence to cognitive forms of 'blindness,' or the inability to effectively multitask.

A study conducted by the National Library of Medicine[2] proved a driver's inability to both drive and talk on a cell phone. The researchers found that drivers using cell phones were at about the same risk of accidents as drunk drivers, missed more than half of the details on the road they would otherwise see, and were twice as likely to fail at noticing stop signs. But here's scary news with all this multitasking: you and your prospective customers could be shrinking

1

important structures in your brains while media multitasking. This is going to impact your selling success, whether you like it or not.

Research by neuroscientists[3] has found that people who use multiple devices simultaneously have lower gray-matter density in an area of the brain associated with cognitive and emotional control. With these new findings, there is increasing concern about how simultaneous multiple media consumption is altering cognition, social-emotional well-being, and brain structure.

Media multitasking is also associated with emotional problems, like anxiety and depression, as well as cognitive problems, like poor attention. In addition, gray matter helps with muscle control, sensory input, decision making, and self-control.

There's more: when you are multitasking and therefore losing gray matter in the brain, it affects the brain's "executive functions." These functions include:

- Judgment
- Analysis
- Organizing
- Problem solving
- Planning
- Creativity

With those "executive functions," the mind codes memories into long-term knowledge. These functions, any of which your prospects need to use when making a purchase decision, are essential to your marketing success.

While there is reason for you, on a personal level, to be concerned about this development, if you're a marketer, you have even more reason to be concerned about your prospective customers. Chances are they're never going to be aware of the risks of losing gray matter. Moreover, many of your prospects will likely ignore it, thinking it will never happen to them.

MOVING DEEPER

People possess fear, uncertainty, and doubt, yet most people like to be uplifted with positive messages. People enjoy uniqueness, and love stories. People are intrigued with interpretation. Further, people desire to be given permission to affirm who they are, their beliefs, and their very existence. Those affirmations—the permission to act—are needed because of emotions.

As human beings, your mind is wired to absorb stimuli in specific ways, and over time, deep memory grooves are created. Your emotions have been formed over a lifetime of experiences, and the resulting personas that people possess belong in one, or a combination, of personality types.

Marketers have opportunities to tap into how the mind works and examine the deep human emotional memories that make each of us tick.

With continuing research, more is understood about how the brain functions than ever before.

THE BRAIN INITIATIVE

The Brain Research through Advancing Innovative Neurotechnologies (BRAIN) Initiative is a research effort intended to revolutionize our understanding of the human mind. The goal is to uncover new ways to treat, prevent, and cure brain disorders like Alzheimer's, schizophrenia, autism, epilepsy, and traumatic brain injury. At first glance, it may seem this has nothing to do with marketing. But the opposite could be true.

Since the BRAIN Initiative was announced in April, 2013, dozens of technology firms, academic institutions, scientists and other key contributors to the field of neuroscience have made significant research commitments. In 2014, $100 million in commitments were announced, and now there is some $300 million in public and private investments[4] already committed.

The momentum for funding the research comes from one disturbing statistic from the World Health Organization[5] and with additional reporting of the economic impact of brain injuries, diseases and disorders in the *Washington Post*:[6]

One in four families worldwide includes someone with a brain injury, disease or disorder, including psychiatric illnesses and developmental disorders, according to the McGovern Institute for Brain Research at the Massachusetts Institute for Technology. In the United States, the economic burden for neurological problems is nearly a half-trillion dollars every year.

The good news is that research is already in progress. The findings and treatment could have a profound influence on the health of people everywhere.

But the findings of these studies could also have an influence on how marketers approach marketing messaging. Studies are already revealing insights about how the brain processes information and makes decisions.

Three benefits of the BRAIN Initiative to marketers are:

1. **Economic Improvement.** When one in four families is impacted with brain injuries or disease, their economical wherewithal or attention to engage with, and respond to our offers is likely diminished. If some of these families are helped, it stands to reason that the entire economy benefits.

2. **What Influences Thinking and Decisions.** By understanding brain function, marketers can better understand the influences of how people think and make decisions. It can also deepen our ability to better imagine personas of our prospective customers.

3. **Focus Marketing Messaging.** By unlocking mind mysteries, findings from research can help marketers focus marketing messaging that connects and resonates more deeply with people, and results in less wasted effort.

The opportunities for individuals, families, our culture and the world will most surely be better because this research promises a better future for us all.

Another outcome of this research is that as more is being learned about the brain, this information is an opportunity for marketers to be smarter. With so much new information and evidence, marketers have an opportunity to better know how the mind works, and use the mind's pathways that can lead to more effective message comprehension to enhance consumer decision-making. Marketers that are uninformed of how memory grooves have been created over a lifetime likely create messages that are too shallow to tap into powerful emotional possibilities.

Contrast shallow messaging with deeper messaging that leads a persona to give oneself permission to act. Before the turn of the 21st century, there wasn't a near-real-time, interactive forum for humans to respond publicly to stimuli. Today, with the Internet and social media in an "always-on" culture, you know when you're liked, followed, shared, and affirmed. The confluence of technology, the Great Recession, and politics has driven us to emotional places that haven't been experienced before in history.

A brief and very general, historical perspective spanning age groups of people who are alive today may help connect why deeper messaging is a requirement for real breakthrough.

As radio and television marketing media emerged, marketers and organizations could market to massive numbers of listeners and viewers in the 1920s on through the Great Depression in the 30s and World War II in the 40s. This impersonalized, one-way mass communication encouraged Americans to consume certain products and services by advertisers. Consumers couldn't "talk back."

Then Baby Boomers dominated the influence of American culture with the massive number of 70 million people born in the 1950s and 1960s. Mass media continued to dominate the landscape. But when the United States Postal Service introduced 5-digit ZIP codes in 1963, targeted selling through direct mail became a more viable and important marketing media option. Credit card availability fueled continued growth of direct mail later in the 1960s, as national credit card systems were created and put into place. The growth of direct mail advertising grew quickly in the 1970s, expanding decade after decade until the late 2000s. Today's opportunity for direct mail is to seamlessly integrate information flow from the printed direct mail piece to online channels (an "o2o" offline to online channel leap).

By the 1980s, computers began to appear in offices, and extended into personal use, leading to expanded consumer demand. In the next decade, the personal computer became more widely found in households. By the 2000s, the Internet enabled consumers and businesses alike to communicate, conduct research, shop, compare, read or watch reviews and testimonials, ask friends for advice, and make purchase decisions differently.

Starting in the mid-2000s, social media was widely introduced, and ultimately became mainstream. This added another layer of liberation for consumers. At last, they could respond and have dialog, sharing their inner thoughts and emotions more publicly. About one-third of people get their news and see major headlines first on social media according to Pew Research[7], as opposed to traditional mass media news channels such as television, radio, newspapers, or magazines.

Even with the multitude of media and channels, many marketers stubbornly hang on to past ways and continue selling as they have in the prior decades, missing the fact that an "always-on" cultural media landscape has changed. Sales messaging over the years have had human emotional components, but even at its best, the messaging often glossed over the deep emotional memory grooves that motivate us to act. Without a methodical process that identifies customer persona, stimulates emotion, calms the mind, positions/repositions, creates story, interprets, and affirms the individual with permission to buy, success can be elusive.

The expansion and accessibility of technology has created a nuanced change in how people interact with messaging, since it's now more apparent how people respond. Marketers have to work harder because of the complex process of how your mind absorbs information and the messaging and communication required to get attention in a noisy, screaming world.

Why is the process more complex today than a decade ago?

The Great Recession that officially started in December of 2007 hit the economy and the psyche of consumers hard. Money was lost in the stock market. Home values plummeted. Spending contracted. Unemployment soared. The dollars consumers spent were more thoughtfully dispensed. Consumers could search for products and services online, read or watch video reviews, and then compare prices from the comfort of their own home.

In addition, politics became even more hardened with "us" versus "them" convictions where "we" and "compromise" have become dirty words. Many factors have increased fear, uncertainty, and doubt. A negative cloud lingers above people's heads.

In a relatively short period of time, the game changed. Many marketers responded to new technologies by trying the latest and greatest marketing device or channel of the month. Other marketers stood on the sidelines, staying the course of what worked a decade ago, hoping that this change in consumer interaction with marketers would pass and revert back to the same way it was in the prior generation.

For many marketers, the basic approach to messaging remains rooted in the past. Some marketers don't yet understand the human reasons, mind pathways and memory grooves of why people respond. Other marketers' approaches haven't evolved with the greater access to virtually every topic imaginable online. In this new century, people—consumers—are empowered. They are more skeptical because of marketer's relentless, bombarding messages. In the attempt to shout louder, the consumer shut marketers out.

The human mind's memory grooves are deeply paved with fear, hope, dreams, and desire for affirmations. But today, consumers are in greater control. They'll call you out on social media and warn the world if they think you're misleading them.

You need to understand and grasp how humans process emotions. Identify the persona. Stimulate, then calm. Position or reposition. Tell your story. Interpret. And set up the tipping point for people to act in your favor, once you move them to give themselves permission to respond. With this process, consumers will reward you with their business and praise, and ultimately can become your advocates.

If you're a marketer using the same techniques that worked a decade ago to generate action, chances are you're experiencing challenging times. Marketing approaches of past times—not all that long ago—don't seem to resonate with consumers as they once did. If they've moved on, you need to as well.

Deeply thinking about how emotion creates motion, I have researched how the mind works through personas, and have looked at the common threads of the most effective messaging. As a result, my marketing recommendations to clients have evolved. I've seen a gradual shift in what engages, endears, and moves people to act.

Ironically, it's the interpretation of big data synced with emotional human reaction that, in my experience, enables certain types of messaging and content to create new memory. Many marketers don't take advantage of accessing the treasure trove of demographic and behavioral data available from data firms. A basic profile is relatively inexpensive. When raw unfiltered data is churned out, it takes a combination of experience and intuition to conjure the persona and identify the emotional triggers of prospective customers and donors.

After more than three decades of writing and overseeing marketing campaigns for hundreds of products in dozens of categories, I've discovered that there is usually a past marketing experience to draw upon that will lead to a sales effort evoking the desired emotional response. And that's why this book was written: to help marketers who may not have had that experience, or who seek a fresh perspective and want to see opportunities through a different lens.

To see the marketing landscape in new ways, consider how these imperatives apply to you.

THREE IMPERATIVES

So how do you recharge marketing approaches and strategies? If current results are disappointing, or worse, in decline, consider these three charges. But I should warn you: If you're a long-time marketer like me, accepting some of these charges might not come easily.

1. Cultivate Your Platform

Long-term success is a result of creating a platform of raving fans, followers, prospects, customers and donors. Your platform is your revenue source. You must grow and cultivate it, whether you're an established organization or a start-up. And you nurture your platform over time by positioning your organization as a trustworthy leader with authority in your market.

If you haven't already, reexamine your organization's persona—and how you're perceived—in the market. You can build (or reinforce) your organization's persona in the marketplace with content marketing tools such as producing videos, writing blogs, and engaging both existing and prospective customers via social media. Even direct mail can include a content writing component with reports, research, and long-form, content-rich letters.

Marketers, especially those in direct response marketing, have had it ingrained for generations that every marketing effort used must deliver a measurable response. Cultivating and investing in the development of a platform, or your list of prospective customers before making a sale, is counter to the culture of approaches like direct marketing. Direct marketers expect every marketing effort to produce a measurable result.

Accepting that content marketing has a place in the marketing mix can be challenging since it normally doesn't deliver a measurable sales response. Yet it often does, in fact, contribute to long-term success. As prospects comb the wide range of media channels available, you must meet them where they are—whether it's at their mailbox, sifting through email, reading a magazine, watching TV, or online while checking social media, viewing videos, or multi-tasking all of the above.

2. How Do You Make Them Feel?

After you meet your customers where they are *physically*, you must engage them *emotionally* using a methodical creative process that tracks what is happening in their mind.

As you considered how to cultivate your platform, you were charged with looking at your organization's persona. Now, imagine the variety of personalities, or personae, of your prospects, customers and donors. The knowledge of who they are dictates how to stir emotions and calm the mind with your solution's message. By establishing who you are with your position, your leadership and unique selling proposition—and using storytelling—you can embed new memory grooves. When the time is right, you interpret your offer for the metaphorical "left brain" part of the mind. The tipping point comes when you intensify the desired emotional "right brain" feeling, so they move themselves with permission to respond.

As you consider how to create feeling in your selling message, heed this quote from Maya Angelou:

> *"I've learned that people will forget what you said, people will forget what you did, but people will never forget how you made them feel."*

Make your customers feel good and connect with them at a level they will always remember.

3. Strategically Monetize

With the charge to cultivate your platform and intensify the emotional feeling in your creative processes, never lose sight of the need to strategically monetize. Your efforts to create fans and followers must have an endgame plan that moves them to become paying customers.

One challenge, for example, is measuring the value of content marketing in the total marketing mix of positioning leadership, establishing authority, and building trust. It may mean that you have to look at the total effect of your numbers in a different way. Your budget may have to blend in the cost of marketing efforts you can't track and average out a cost-per-order based on all activity. Consider carving out a separate budget for content and other hard-to-track efforts. You might look at those costs as a branding expense or as part of overhead.

Now may be the time to view certain types of marketing activities as contributing to your overall success without specific attribution to a sale. By my own admission, as a classically trained direct marketer, this has been a tough concept for me to accept.

If your marketing is delivering great results, by all means, stay the course, but remain vigilant for trends and tools that may prove valuable. But if response is lackluster or declining, consider that the days of profitably casting out a pitch to buy a product that's unknown, without trust, credibility or authority, have passed.

Your success includes the charge to build and cultivate a platform of prospective customers. The imperative includes communicating a deeper, more cerebral approach that impacts memory and swells the emotional feelings inside your current and prospective customers' minds (which is what this book is about). And as you calculate bottom-line profitability, you may have to rethink how you budget and monetize.

CHAPTER 2

MIND MYSTERIES

I have lived with a mysterious obsessive-compulsive disorder since the age of 6. Consuming me since I was a child, I have a natural curiosity of how and why the mind is wired and works as it does.

MY STORY OF FEELING ALONE

Growing up, I felt alone. The compulsive, and uncommon, disorder that has highly influenced my life comes with a rather unflattering name: trichotillomania, or compulsive hair pulling. I thought I was the only person in the world who pulled my hair while growing up. The medical and psychiatric communities estimate that perhaps 2 percent of all children will pull noticeable clumps of hair, with many of us going on to become adults still dealing with the disorder. Most of us live with the disorder in silence and full of shame. I was no different. But in 2007, I resolved to go public with my disorder, shave my head, lifting decades of burden from my shoulders. It was a liberating decision that has led me to this point in my life. I wrote a book, titled *Urges*, about my childhood of living with this disorder, published in 2009.

Knowing my brain was different from others, I've always wanted to peer inside and see if a wire was crossed. I dreamed that my brain could be opened up, the misguided wire that created those urges to pull hair would be gently moved to its proper place, and that I would stop pulling and my life would be normal, just like everyone else.

But of course, the brain can't be opened and misconnected wires and pathways uncrossed to change the code. And of course, a "normal" brain is a matter of perspective. The fact is that everyone is different; every individual on earth has life experiences that have propelled them to where they are today, and those experiences have created an individual persona.

Having a hair pulling disorder has indelibly altered my perspective of people around me. When I'm in public places, like the coffee shop where I'm writing this, I see people with "comment boxes" floating above them giving me an insight into their persona.

For example, I wonder why the guy at the next table is wearing a ball cap backwards, and why his neck, arms and hands are covered with tattoos. He's boasting loudly to his buddies who are there to hear him. He's holding court. It's apparent he's a body builder and wrestler (as are the guys with him). Was the "mean guy" look a way to boost his self-image? No one knows. But if you're a marketer, you have to ask yourself what this suggests about the sales messaging needed to motivate this guy. Clearly, he requires a specific approach that corresponds with his mindset to get him to act.

At another table, the woman who is dressed to the nines is obviously consumed with looking good and turning heads. What is her deeper emotional reason and persona? Does beauty help to boost her self-image, thus creating her special persona? Moreover, as a marketer, how do you stimulate her emotion, calm her mind, create a positioning statement she will buy into, share a story that will engage her, interpret this for her, and ultimately help her conclude that she has permission to buy or act? Her mind pathways are the same as the bodybuilder, but what's inside each memory groove is decidedly different.

Finally, the elderly lady at another table is talking loudly, probably because of hearing loss. You have to remember that outward appearances and actions are often a reflection of a physical state. But this physical state deeply influences an individual's persona. Just as the elderly lady is affected by her hearing issues, I was affected because of pulling my hair. I was ashamed. I compensated for my appearance then, and probably do still somewhat today, by a desire—obsession, really—to look good in other ways to divert attention away from my weakness.

I could go on and on, but the point should be clear: everyone has a specific persona that is the core of their lives and existence. My observation, after decades of creating marketing messaging, is that there are 12 primary personas. There can be secondary personas, individualized to certain sets of characteristics, but this core group forms a basis for a place to start and can be tailored for your situation.

UNDERSTANDING THE EMOTIONAL CONTROL PANEL

Marketers must understand the personas—the emotional control panel as I sometimes call it—of prospective customers or donors. Failing to do so will result with blending in with the sound of the coffee shop, instead of standing apart and creating results.

A few years ago, I had a client who said he never wanted to test around the edges. He wanted to only test big and bold things, such as a brand new position or unique selling proposition. That's what we did, and we have the results to prove that these big and bold ideas moved the needle (in this case, a sales increase of 60%).

But getting to 60% wasn't easy. It took a few hits and misses. And it took a few years, truthfully. It was after talking with prospective customers in focus groups in individual conversations that we could better discern the underlying mood.

The product we were selling was fruitcake. Decades ago, an entire generation of people loved to give fruitcake to friends or business associates as Christmas gifts. It was a product that was easily shipped worldwide. But after years of being the butt of jokes, a stigma set in about fruitcake.

During our focus groups, we asked the participants (who had never tasted this brand of fruitcake) to sample it. One person after another remarked how good it tasted. It was nothing like what they expected. A recurring bit of advice they kept telling us was to change the name of the product from "fruitcake" to something else. Why? "Fruitcake" as a broad category, had accumulated generally unfavorable connotations. There was a stigma around buying fruitcake, and there was an even larger stigma of giving fruitcake as a gift.

What they were really saying was "give me permission to buy something else," and they would do just that. They wouldn't be embarrassed, and their social standing would stay intact. So, we repositioned the name to "Native Texas Pecan Cakes," and sales soared higher by 60% from new customers. Interestingly, the repositioning didn't really move the needle as much for existing customers, but perhaps that was to be expected. As customers, they didn't need a repositioning to give themselves permission to buy. They had already made that decision, based on previous marketing campaigns.

Or consider another example how getting to the deeper emotion triggered a sales increase of 35% for an insurance company. Who wants to buy life insurance? Few would say they "want" life insurance, but most of us know we "need" the financial protection life insurance offers.

We needed to give the prospect permission, in their minds, to buy life insurance because it affirms something in their deeper emotion. In this instance, the insight and permission to buy arose from an analysis of the data. After looking at the demographic and interest attributes of those who had previously purchased the life insurance plan, these characteristics became amplified:

- The buyer was a woman in her late 50s.
- Her interest in her grandchildren was high.
- She read the Bible and devotions.

This grandmother probably cared more about her grandchildren than for a husband (that's assuming she was married; many were single or widowed). Add the notion that if she was married, she probably assumed she would outlive her husband. But she cared deeply about her grandchildren. She liked to play games and contests. And since she read the Bible and devotions, we ventured that perhaps she wanted to leave a legacy. Whether that legacy was with money being given to a grandchild or leaving money to a favorite charity, this deeper repositioning of the message worked and sales increased by 35%.

GETTING TO 35% OR 60% SALES INCREASES

These are just a couple examples of breaking from tired messaging and using a marketing and sales messaging that moved the prospective buyer to an emotional place, closer to giving self-permission. There are a few common threads between these stories that can be applied to every marketer so that you can take the deeper dive to understanding a core customer's persona.

1. Talk to customers one-on-one when you can, even if by phone.

2. Get a dozen of your prospective customers, clients, or donors in a room and, using an experienced moderator, ask the deeper questions in a focus group.

3. Profile your customers by overlaying demographic and behavior information. You'll gain tremendous insights, but you must pause and interpret the data. Reading it isn't enough. Discuss it, and then write the report, complete with charts and graphs, to amplify the findings, so others can readily grasp them.

4. If warranted, rename your product, and rebrand. Change the design. Be bold!

5. Use storytelling techniques to create a new memory. Story has been effectively used in sales, speeches, sermons, and other presentations for centuries. It works and is often under-utilized.

6. Interpret what gives your prospective customer a good feeling about owning your product. Translate features into benefits. Use testimonials or reviews. Assure the individual through a strong satisfaction guarantee.

7. Identify the permission that prospects must give themselves so they become customers, and affirm it with a deeper message. Identifying the permission may require testing, but through creativity and based on the persona, you should be able to quickly imagine the level of permission required to move the individual to action.

CHAPTER 3

THE SEVEN PATHWAYS

Through research and results from sales campaigns, it's possible to infer how the mind sequentially processes information. In mere seconds, your message zips past a filter into a mental folder. The first folder can reject your message outright without consideration. Another folder allows for a few more seconds of consideration. And still another folder will process the information—your content and sales message—for more scrutiny. Get to this deeper folder, and now you've opened up to your possibilities to move the prospective customer to creating a new long-term memory.

Understand the code on the passageway and the folders that your mind goes through, and you can crack the code on strengthening your message's effectiveness.

The list below aligns specific brain functions and what is needed to breakthrough in each of the seven mind pathways. I will explain each of these pathways in more detail in the following chapters. But for now, this list provides you an overview of what you will discover in the chapters ahead.

1. IDENTIFY THE PERSON

This is foundational to your success. You define the persona of the prospect you want to move to becoming your customer or donor.

It's vital that we understand the basis of the personality (or persona) of the audience so we can relevantly communicate and be aligned with how the mind thinks. To get to the persona of our prospective customer we must dig deeper than basic demographics, lifestyles or interests.

In ancient Latin, the word persona meant "mask." And "mask" is an interesting metaphor as we think about an individual's persona, because people often place a mask over their true personality. Peel it off, and we may expose emotions surprisingly different than what we would have expected.

Breaking through requires that we think deeply about our customer and give them a reason why they should listen to us. While it's helpful to know underlying demographics and interests about our customer, those are not likely the tipping points that lead to a prospect becoming a customer.

2. STIMULATE EMOTION

Now that you have a clear view of the persona of your prospective customer, you must stimulate emotion and get attention. The brain has a filter, or radar, between the conscious and subconscious mind. It's called the Reticular Activating System (RAS). The RAS filters the incoming information and affects what you pay attention to, what arouses you, and what will not get access to all of your brain. Before messages can gain entry to your higher, thinking mind, the RAS assesses input.

If your prospect is stressing from negative emotions (a natural tendency for most people), he or she will react instinctively as the "reactive mind" processes your message sending the data right to the amygdala—the primal part of the brain that reacts in "fight or flight" mode. The amygdala, sometimes called "lizard brain" because of its role to regulate reaction to threats to life, has an evolutionary purpose for humans to survive and pass on genetic information through reproduction.

The amygdala reacts in a "fight" or "flight" mode. When you encounter sudden danger, you might freeze, your blood pressure and heart rate may begin to rise, with the release of stress hormones. The amygdala initiates all of these reactions.

The amygdala stimulates the most inner, fundamental human emotion of anger, safety, or desire for reproduction. When this powerful intuitive response kicks in, the rest of your brain shuts down. In contrast, positivity stimulates optimism to continue to engage. Stimulate emotion to get attention, but then you must move your prospect quickly to a place that calms the mind.

3. CALM THE MIND

Now your opportunity is to calm and assure your prospects there is a relevant solution to the threat, or the suggestion of fear, uncertainty or doubt. When the emotion is positive, the mind is instantly put at ease with neurotransmitters. Neurotransmitters are the brain chemicals that communicate information throughout our brain and body. Neurotransmitter chemicals include dopamine which delivers pleasure through reward; serotonin that invokes memory and opens up the mind to learning, and norepinephrine, which is necessary to moderate mood. You want to quickly active these brain chemicals.

4. POSITION / REPOSITION WITH A UNIQUE SELLING PROPOSITION

When the cocktail of neurotransmitters mix, short-term memory grooves are initiated. Short-term memory grooves can be created by effectively communicating a positioning statement, or unique selling proposition (USP). With a USP, the mind's attention holds longer. When you effectively position who you are, or how your product or service is unique, apart from competitors, you improve your chances of acceptance into your prospects deeper thinking mind. New short-term memory that is converted to long-term memory is essential for a marketer to build trust and lead up to closing a sale. And new long-term memory can be more easily made with a USP or repositioning of an existing product or an organization.

5. TELL A STORY

You start a new memory groove with your positioning through a USP, so now you move to deepen the groove with storytelling. When using story, you are better able to deepen the groove of a new memory into long-term memory in the hippocampus. The hippocampus is a small region of the brain that forms part of the limbic system and is primarily associated with memory. It takes sensory inputs and integrates them with relational or associational patterns. It plays a very important role in storing your memories and connecting them to your emotions. With an engaging story and a USP, you can magnetically pull the individual into the storyline so they are a participant, actively seeing themselves in the role as a customer. This creates a new perspective, memory, and deepens grooves in the brain for recall.

6. INTERPRET

Upon presenting your USP and strengthening it with story, you're ready to move to the brain's logical part of the thinking, the metaphorical left brain. The marketer can now interpret features to benefits, introduce price and make comparisons with the competition. Your message must interpret the outcome for the individual to deepen the memory grooves. Any product or service skepticism must be dealt with here. In this stage, you introduce the financial cost and present it with the return on investment and value component. Testimonials or reviews from consumers about your product or organization solidify the message even more. These reassure the individual through a strong guarantee of satisfaction.

7. PERMISSION TO ACT

After your sales presentation has been logically made, you take your prospective customer or donor back to emotion, the metaphorical right brain. Here, you overlay the newly established memory grooves with an emotional appeal. You must be careful here that a gut reaction that's not in your favor doesn't prevail. You've used a combination of emotional and logical persuasion throughout this process, but now you need to seal the deal by focusing on an emotional persuasion component. Now you should lead the prospective customer to say to themselves "this is good, this is smart, I give myself permission to act/buy/respond/contribute."

By now, you may be wondering how you can apply this flow to your situation.

One way to overcome this concern is an exercise where you fill in the blanks with information about how you would approach each of these pathways of the mind to create new grooves. Using the example of marketing fruitcake and insurance, discussed earlier, here is a table that will give you an idea of how mapping out these processes work.

Fruitcake

1. **Identify the Persona**. Your prospect's personal brand and social standing are reflected in the gifts they give.
2. **Stimulate Emotion.** Discovery of a uniquely baked gift.
3. **Calm the Mind.** It's a product enjoyed for generations by people from around the world.
4. **Position / Reposition.** A unique product, unavailable in stores, has a fascinating story about its origins and why it tastes different than any other product.
5. **Tell a Story.** The pecans for this cake are native to trees in Texas and the South along certain rivers and streams with ideal soil conditions. These are trees that grow to 150 feet in height, were seedlings at the time of the Civil War, and are majestic trees still standing today.
6. **Interpret.** Your friends will be delighted with a delicious unique gift. Your complete satisfaction is guaranteed or your money back.
7. **Permission to Act.** My social standing will be preserved, or enhanced, because I thoughtfully gave this unique product.

Life Insurance

1. **Identify the Persona.** I need financial protection for my family, and I want to leave a memorable, usable lasting legacy for my loved ones.
2. **Stimulate Emotion.** How will my loved ones pay for my funeral and live day-to-day if I suddenly die?
3. **Calm the Mind.** I can leave a financial gift that my loved ones can use to help ease the pain of my passing.
4. **Position / Reposition.** There is a guarantee of my eligibility and I don't have to endure an embarrassing and invasive medical exam.
5. **Tell a Story.** I can see how others benefit from the peace-of-mind of life insurance, and hear from beneficiaries how they were able to move on with their lives after the passing of a loved one.
6. **Interpret.** Detailed information on features and benefits of this policy helps me understand why I need this insurance.

7. **Permission to Act.** For about the cost of a daily cup of coffee, I can financially help my loved ones and leave a legacy of my life.

Now that you've seen the framework for this process, you can create your own matrix using these examples.

Let's now take a deeper dive into each of these seven pathways in the next seven chapters to more deeply create new memory grooves in the mind.

CHAPTER 4
#1 IDENTIFY THE PERSONA

Persona

Stimulate

Calm

Position

Story

Interpret

Permission

The persona of your consumer is deeper than basic demographics and lifestyles or interests. In ancient Latin, the word persona meant "mask."

The word "mask" is an interesting metaphor for persona. People often place a mask on their true personality. Peel it off, and you may expose emotions different than what you would have expected. I'll use myself as an example. I shared with you earlier that as a child I lived with the mysterious compulsive disorder of hair pulling. By the time I turned 21 and had my first job after graduating, the stress of leaving college and transitioning to my career began to overwhelm me. After only a couple of months on the job, I was horrified to see clumps of hair on my desk or on the floor around my desk as a result of the uncontrollable urge to pull.

But I would never have admitted then that I was a hair puller, even though the evidence both on my desk and the floor, along with bald spots on my head, exposed the truth. My mask would have been to blame someone else and live in denial about what was going on. So, for me, doing whatever it took to cover up the truth was essential. That's why only a couple of months into my job, I took the first step of calling a men's hair salon where they sold hairpieces. I could literally cover-up the damage, and in the process, calm my urge to pull my hair. I wore a hairpiece from the time I was 21 until I turned 50.

Herein lays the challenge for marketers: people often wear a mask because people don't want truths about them to be exposed. Yet, as marketers, you know there are emotions underneath, and when your content and messaging makes its way deeper inside, the mask is lifted and you're invited to delve further inside the mind.

What's behind the mask is a personality that has been formulated over a lifetime. It's said that people are an accumulation of life experiences. I think of the mind—and emotions—as having a complex fabric of weaves that crisscross each other to form different textures, colors, and sensitivities.

WHAT, HOW, AND WHY

As marketers, you might consider the people you're selling to as your target market. But you're selling to people, not targets. To generate response, it's essential to understand underlying demographics and interests about your customer. While this is a starting point, it's not likely the tipping point that leads to a prospect becoming a customer or donor. Breaking through requires that you think deeply about your customer and lead them to the answer of "why" they should respond to you instead of a competitor or no one at all.

A thought-provoking TED Talk video of author Simon Sinek, titled "How Great Leaders Inspire Action,"[8] elegantly speaks about the importance of the "why." The title of this video (available to view at CustomerMindCode.com/Resources) could just as well have been "How Great Marketers Inspire Action." Sinek describes concentric, ever-narrowing golden circles of "what," "how" and "why." The outside ring, where most marketers approach customers and prospects, is the "what." The middle ring is the "how." Marketers usually excel at filling in the "what" and "how," as features are translated into benefits for the logical part of the brain.

But at the core of the golden circle, where decisions are often made in the brain, is the "why." It's the emotional response. If your messaging isn't working, there is a challenge for you to think more deeply about the "why" of your organization and your product or service. Reach this point, and you can tap more deeply into the emotion of your prospect.

FALLING SHORT OF EXPECTATIONS

Knowing what your customers really want and creating a profile are essential for any company, but brands are often falling short of expectations. The importance of knowing your customer base is further reinforced through a relevant example. In 2011, a new and experienced Chief Executive Officer was hired to head JC Penney. Within a month, he launched a radical rebranding strategy that upended the look, feel, and merchandise of the store. This radicalization of the brand didn't reflect what the consumers wanted and collapsed sales within months.

The CEO was later quoted to say that "Our core customer, I think, was much more dependent and enjoyed coupons more than I understood."[9] He didn't have a clear picture of his customer's persona, which was a person who liked special ways to save, such as coupons and markdowns. Looking at your customers' behavioral drivers, obstacles to purchasing, and mindset can enable you to understand your customer better.

THEORY OF EMOTION

There are numerous theories of emotion and general emotional responses. Those emotions include, but aren't limited to:

- Anger
- Fear
- Sadness
- Hatred
- Hope
- Trust
- Happiness

These emotions are part of your wiring.

There are five broadly based personality types, as reported in *Psychology Today*[10] that are molded over a lifetime. Read these and do two things: First, using a bit of self-analysis, which of these five types do you consider reflective of your personality? Second, consider which of these five best describes your customer. Consider, too, that it's possible a person may cross into different types, but generally, one type will be the most dominant for an individual:

1. **Extraversion,** which refers to the general degree of positivity, approach motivation, and sociability.
2. **Neuroticism,** which refers to the general degree of negativity, avoidance motivation, and emotional reactivity.
3. **Agreeableness,** which refers to the tendency to get along, be warm, sympathetic and understanding (the opposite of paranoid hostility).
4. **Conscientiousness,** which refers to the extent of organized planning, responsibility, and achievement motivation.
5. **Openness,** which refers to the desire to experience novelty, connect with new feelings, and learn new things.

While this is a place to start, these five broad categories don't tell the full story of the persona of your best customer or donor. You must drill down from these broad factors to more defined personas that describe your customer (or donor), and prospective customer (or donor).

CREATING A PERSONA

The persona goes beyond demographic and behavior information. It gets to the intuition and core thinking of the fears, hopes, dreams, and values of an individual.

Creating a persona requires work on your behalf, but is prerequisite to achieving maximum marketing success. It requires you to more deeply think about your audience, and having personas will make you a stronger marketer. Do the work. It's foundational. You must have this first piece of the seven-step process established for the next six steps to work.

A strongly developed persona will channel you to creating more relevant messages that engage. When you're forced to get into the character of the person you're selling, you better understand the genuine thoughts, feelings, and behaviors of your prospective customers. Not only does it make your message more relevant, but it also makes your message more engaging. With engagement comes your chance to make the sale. When your prospect becomes a buyer, you have an opportunity to create a raving fan who shares your message and helps do your selling for you.

A persona is more than just a description of a person. Personas are fictional characters that comprise needs, goals, and behavioral patterns among your prospects, customers and donors.

When you create a persona, you are more strategic in homing in your message to your audience. You identify and internalize their deep inner thinking and value, and more importantly, you illustrate in your marketing message that you understand who they are as human beings and what makes them tick.

As you succeed at creating the persona, you also discover opportunities. Those opportunities can positively impact your product, service, or organization.

Creating a persona will help you, the marketing team, and internal staff focus on your organization's goals. Benefits may include:

- Leaders and executive management having a better understanding of your target market.
- Copywriters writing for the appropriate audience with a stronger, suitably toned message.
- Designers having a better feel for how to convey the graphic appeal around your message.

ELEMENTS OF A PERSONA

You will generally want to include information such as:

- Fictional person's name, e.g., Cathy Compassion, Susie Show-off, Macho Mike.
- Demographics (age, education, ethnicity, and family status).
- Behavioral information and interests.
- Priorities in their lives.
- A statement, written in the first person that sums up what matters most to this individual.

- Stock photos of people who might embody your persona to make the person feel more real.
- Job titles and major responsibilities (for business-to-business).

RESEARCH

Without research, your foundation for creating a persona will be weak. You most likely have a good handle on your current and prospective customers, yet sometimes there are nuances overlooked that, once identified, can propel your messaging to greater success.

There are several methods to research the persona of your prospective customer or donor.

In-Person Interviews. Get on the phone and talk to customers. Ask them questions beyond the superficial (examples appear later in this chapter). Don't hide behind email. Call them and interact with follow-up questions to dig deeper.

Focus Groups. This format allows a good exchange of ideas. Usually, you have a dozen people in a room, with a moderator asking a set of questions to each individual or the entire group. Over the years as a copywriter and analyst, I have moderated focus groups to gain valuable insights. A professional focus group facility is recommended, where you and creative staff can observe the conversation behind a glass wall and not seen by the participants. Bring the product so individuals can see, use or taste it. One challenge of focus groups is that sometimes one individual takes on the role of spokesperson for the group. While the moderator is responsible for controlling that environment, inevitably it can happen, and when it does, sometimes the comments from participants are skewed to agree with the self-anointed spokesperson. An approach I've used is to hand out a printed questionnaire that each person can answer at the end. A written questionnaire gives participants the opportunity to speak their own minds, and can be a source of more reliable data. One more thing to remember if you use focus groups: what people tell you, and what people actually do, are often two different things. The discussion often reveals a confirmation of what you already believed, but new ideas can emerge. Focus groups are costly, so it is essential you have a plan and work with a reputable moderator and facility.

Online Research. Set up an online survey using any of the services online (some are free), load your customer email list to the website, and you'll get answers quickly and inexpensively.

Profile. Many of the leading data firms and credit bureaus offer profiles of customers. Often, a profile comes with a model used to identify prospective customers. But if you don't model your customers, you can still get a profile, and usually at an affordable cost. The profile you seek needs to have demographic, psychographic and behavioral purchase data. The profile report is often hundreds of pages that index your customers as either above or below the average score of all consumers in America. You'll find out if people enjoy any of the "Seven F's" (Family, Friends, Fun, Food, Fashion, Fitness, or Fido/Felines) and potentially hundreds of attributes. Some models I've found of help, as referenced in an earlier chapter, have been identified a customer as a woman in her 50s, whose interest is in her grandchildren, enjoys Bible and devotional reading, and playing contests. If you have a profile generated, there is one vital last step you must undertake. You must look at the hundreds of pages of data (sometimes in charts), and identify the top three to five attributes that distinguish your customers from everyone else. Then analyze the information and write your report with an eye toward how your findings would be used in marketing.

Interview Your Team. If you have salespeople, talk to them. Talk to your customer service people who answer phone calls, and anyone else in your organization that interacts with your customers and get their perspective on what they believe are your customers' primary values.

Website Analytics. You will be surprised what you can learn from online sources. Start by looking at the analytics of visitors to your website. Of course, this information could be skewed if your customer doesn't visit your website. But for those who visit your website, you have access to a treasure trove of analytic information. You can discover, for instance, keywords used to find your website (which might be the magic words you use in your copy and messaging), along with the pages they view most, or how they found your website.

Website Services. Alexa.com and Quantcast.com (among others) are websites that enable you to learn the characteristics of those going to your website (keep in mind, visitors aren't always customers). If you want to know about your competitors, you can check out who visits their websites and conduct a competitive analysis. Alexa.com is a great resource to learn about traffic, engagement, reputation metrics, demographics, and more. The basic service is free, but for a monthly fee you get additional information about your competitors. When you want to compare the demographics of who comes to your site versus your competitors, go to Quantcast.com. You'll be shown an index of how a website performs compared to the Internet average. You'll get statistics on attributes such as age, presence of children, income, education, and ethnicity.

Social Media Sentiment Analysis. Ask questions of your followers. Encourage them to comment. The answers might not always be what you want to read, but transparency and owning up to the occasional "fail" openly will earn you credibility and inform you of opportunity areas in which to improve. Facebook has data on your customers, such as age, location, and engagement with your Facebook page (assuming that you have one). Look at Twitter streams. If you're a business-to-business marketer, use LinkedIn. There are many other social media outlets you can (and should) monitor to better understand customer passions.

No Customers Yet. If you don't have many customers, or your business is new, look at your competitors (using some of the steps described above). Read their websites and blogs. Importantly, read comments on blogs for insights and thinking from their followers and customers.

BASIC CHARACTERISTICS

Identifying basic characteristics, needs, and wants, is a good and easy place to start. Using real data is best. If you don't have access to real data, use your best estimate, and start by listing these attributes:

Personal
- Age range
- Gender
- Presence of children or grandchildren (and their ages)
- Highest level of education
- Household income

- Education level attained
- Professional
- Blue-Collar
- Retired

Priorities
- Priority in life
- How you help keep that priority in balance
- How you help solve challenges that conflict with priorities
- Values
- Fears in the way of meeting priorities

BUILDING BLOCKS TO CREATE A PERSONA

Once you've conducted your research, you're ready to start creating personas for your organization. Here are a few steps you'll want to undertake as you move forward from here.

- **Condense Your Research.** Hopefully you have engaged in at least two or three of the research options described above. Comparing information from different sources will challenge you to look carefully at your customers. As you do this, observe characteristics that are relevant to you and your product, as well as those that are specific.
- **Brainstorm.** Get your team together to discuss the findings of your research. Remember: in brainstorming there are no bad ideas!
- **Traits.** Start a list of traits that identify the character of this individual. Are they shoppers? High-level executives? What do they like?
- **Multiple Personas.** By now, you may realize that you're dealing with more than just one persona. Chances are you'll need to create additional personas. It's completely reasonable to identify three-to-five different types of buyers.
- **Make Them Real.** As you drill down into more information, choose a person's name to represent your emerging first persona. Describe the background and values of the individual. Find stock photos that

might look like the person you're describing. This will take persona development to a stronger level now that you can visually see someone as your customer.

- **Write. Revise. Revise Again.** You might begin by writing the persona in the third person. Test it by rewriting it in the first person so it's your prospective customer who is telling the story about themselves, their values, and their expectations from your product, service, or organization. If you're a B-to-B organization, add a job title and role inside a company.

- **Visualize How They See You.** Your persona should now drill down to more psychological detail so you see their view of you through their lens. This topic will be explored more fully in the next section.

DEEPER INSIDE YOUR PERSONA'S THOUGHTS

So, you've started thinking about your customers and prospective customers in terms of basic demographic interests.

Now the fun part begins: imagining what is deep inside their mind as values, fears, hopes and dreams. Your intuition is essential. Place yourself in the mind of your customer and approach how you view them with empathy. To get to this part of the imagination process, you might start by posing these questions to yourself, and in a team brainstorming setting.

- What is important to your prospect as it relates to your product, service or organization?
- Do your customers want something new?
- What is in the way of your prospect's decision to change?
- What could motivate your customer to buy from you?
- What do they need to know to make a decision?
- What is their pain (emotional and/or physical)?
- Where do they go for information or advice?

As you complete your persona, having written it in third person, and then in first person, let your current or prospective customer tell their story.

Give them a voice and a platform, and you'll see your customers from a different perspective.

12 FOUNDATIONAL PERSONAS

Having created messages for campaigns reaching tens of millions of households worldwide, it's my observation there are 12 foundational personas. Usually one of these is the dominant persona, but occasionally two or three can be blended for a more universal view of your most likely customer. Chances are, too, that you'll want to modify these or you'll decide that your product or service has its own distinctive persona. What's most important is that you take the first step to identify the personality of your customer.

The 12 personas I've observed most often are:

- Trailblazers/Early Adopters
- My Brand/My Lifestyle/My Growth
- Money Matters
- On Financial Edge
- Right Thing to Do: Taking the High Road
- Love and Social Relationships
- Adrenaline Seekers: Opportunists
- Safe Players
- Hiding My Compulsion
- Fifty Plus
- Business 8 to 5
- Did I Matter?

The core values of each of these personas follow.

1. TRAILBLAZERS/EARLY ADOPTERS

Deep down, I yearn to be the first to acquire what's new. I'm an "innovator." I thrive on blazing a new trail with what's new and cutting edge. I will stand in line for hours to be the first to acquire the latest, greatest, and newest product as it is being introduced. Ahead of the curve? That's me! It makes me feel important. Some call me a geek.

I have the money and financial means to be ahead of the pack. Yeah, I know the prices are often higher to be the first to have it. But it's worth it to me. I want to be the first to have everything, so that I can flash it around.

I'm passionate and deeply desire to be among the few in the know so I can acquire it first. And when I find something new and cool that I really like, you can bet I'm going to advocate the product and become an evangelist for the product creator. But companies should beware: if the product sucks, I'll tell the world. I'm always online, chatting, posting, and making my opinion known. My friends and I stick together to alert everyone of product fails.

2. MY BRAND/MY LIFESTYLE/MY GROWTH

My personal brand demands attention. My look, lifestyle, and personal growth they are all at the core of my being. The fact is when I receive a compliment of any kind, my head swells with pride. I love to be glitzy glamorous, and when I'm flattered, it reinforces that I am eternally young. You might call me a fashionista. If looking good above all else means being physically uncomfortable, then that's the way it is.

I'm comfortable spending money, so I can brag about the experience. My lifestyle choices and brand are made to position myself as the envy of people around me. I want to imagine myself as a jet setter who travels extensively and who dresses the part.

It's also important to me that I grow my mind and my skills because knowledge is highly valued and is a part of my personal brand. Possessing an intellectual acumen for leadership positions me as someone who is important.

3. MONEY MATTERS

I'm a practical and sensible person. I have common sense. My decisions are usually based on a combination of price and value. I don't always look for the lowest price in every situation, but I do look for the greatest value, and I'm careful with my money. I'm frugal. I work hard. I don't believe in needlessly spending my money. I don't need thrills or frills. Most important to me is accumulating money, not possessions.

I wish the world were more sensible. I know I can't change the world, but I think I can be of influence to people around me. How I spend money becomes a badge that I wear on my sleeve. Don't misunderstand me; I'm not seeking notoriety. I really don't even seek attention. Rather, I quietly lead my life with a certain smugness that will ultimately enable me to live comfortably. I don't want the financial pressures that so many people feel. For me, money matters a lot. I will seek out the greatest value I can find, and I will be quietly proud of my accomplishment.

4. ON FINANCIAL EDGE

I always feel strapped. My credit isn't very good. I often don't fit in to traditional financial services and banking. Unfortunately I'm not always able to pay my bills on time.

It's a struggle. I'm not proud of my situation, but I do the best I can to manage my finances. Sometimes I just overspend. I'm not good at math. I guess my reading skills aren't so good either. I don't tend to pay a lot of attention to accountability. I go about my life not realizing that I have exhausted all of the money available to me. Other times it's just that I don't make enough money to pay all the bills. As the saying goes, "there's too much month left at the end of the money."

I'll admit I don't know how to manage money. It wasn't taught to me. Or maybe I just wasn't paying attention in school.

I'm doing my best, but I sometimes fall short of what the world expects of me. I live paycheck to paycheck. I'm afraid of people taking advantage of me, yet I'm often open to helping others just like me. I'm part of my silent community. That's my life and I struggle to make changes and improvements to my standard of living.

5. RIGHT THING TO DO: TAKING THE HIGH ROAD

I'm a person who takes the high road. I make decisions based on what are right for me, my family, my health, the environment, and more. My persona is one who judges and makes decisions that are based on if a product or cause supports my belief system of doing the right thing. Sometimes I will fall on a sword for any cause. Some say I'm an activist.

I believe every decision should be based on if it's the right choice to support whatever deep-seated values I possess. A decision must support my belief system, or I will have misgivings and buyer's remorse. I feel affirmed when decisions give me permission to feel good about myself, the people around me, the earth, and our culture.

I recycle. I try to choose food that is nutritious or organic, and grown with as little negative impact on the earth as possible. I drive a fuel-efficient vehicle. In the back of my mind, I must know that my purchase decisions won't have a negative impact on culture or the world around me. I want to see, from marketers, how their product is the right choice for me. Cost isn't always an issue.

The world and our culture will spiral downward unless we all participate in turning things around. I don't want to have any regrets. I will do my part. I wish other people would share my sentiments. I'm fearful we will leave the world in a worse place than it was given to us. My righteous-based decisions are my small way of making myself and the world a better place. I sleep better at night when I have taken the high road.

6. LOVE AND SOCIAL RELATIONSHIPS

My life revolves around relationships. I am affirmed by love and acceptance from loved ones, family and friends. I'll admit that sometimes I'm insecure about myself. I highly value being loved, wanted and desired. I need to have a partner in my life to feel fulfilled. When that happens, all is well in the world. Without a life partner, there is emptiness that I crave to have filled. I turn to family and friends to fill that void. The center of my life is to be liked, and I seek affirmations for everything I do.

My purchase decisions are influenced by what my friends will think about me. I am naturally attracted to anything that could make me more lovable and likable to others. I love being active on social media. I am careful about the photos I post because I want them to be a statement about me. Selfies with influential people are important to me, and I will regularly post about those experiences. It affirms who I am and it elevates my self-worth.

7. ADRENALINE SEEKERS: OPPORTUNISTS

I am convinced that I can beat the system. Whenever there is an opportunity or chance that I will prevail "over the man," I experience a physical adrenaline rush. Money isn't the big motivator. Feeling that I can beat the system or beat the house—whether it's the stock market or a casino—gives me a rush like none other.

I can smell opportunity, and I play to win. Money is a scorecard. I don't always need to win a big pile of cash; I just need to score. A small win is still a win, and it's worthy of bragging rights. I'm a realist, but I'm also a dreamer. I like to be given the opportunity to see myself as part of the story and dream big because when that happens, my adrenaline motivates me to play along.

I'm a risk taker and I crave winning. Losing isn't taken easily, but it happens. However, you're not going to hear about any of my losses. My losses are quickly erased from my memory grooves and they're replaced with the memory of past wins. Adrenaline gushes when I'm introduced to an opportunity that I sense is an alternative to traditional approaches.

8. SAFE PLAYERS

I play my life safely. I don't like to take risks. For that reason, I'm often sought after by my risk-taking friends because I am a problem solver. I think of myself as unassuming in my approach to buying decisions. Financial risks are out of the question. All my earthly possessions are important to me, and I protect and nurture them. I am fearful of making a decision that will result in loss, and losses aren't limited to only money. As a professional, my belief in safety extends into my relationships with clients. I'll admit that I am more pessimistic than optimistic about outcomes. I tend to doubt some choices that I make, so I approach things very carefully.

I am inclined to create a firewall around myself so that I don't have to deal with problems. I think of myself as a problem solver. I am loyal to organizations that help keep me safe.

9. HIDING MY COMPULSION

I have deep-seated compulsions that need to be regularly fed. Usually I hide them. I'm aware of my compulsions and how destructive they can be to me, both physically and mentally. I yearn for normalcy and continually seek out how to lead a normal life. Secrecy is paramount. Anything I see from marketers must be discreet and private. I want to see support from organizations about what can be done to help what eats away at my core.

There are dozens, probably hundreds, of niche compulsions like mine. Some of those compulsions are painfully apparent and obvious to people, yet some are not. The key for a marketer is to respect my boundaries and barriers. For them to break through requires a certain degree of sensitivity. They must build trust and empathy. It will take time and it will require proof. I'm unlikely to reach out to peers for advice or recommendations, so my social interaction is kept to a minimum. But once an organization has earned my trust, I will be loyal to the core.

10. FIFTY PLUS

I may be over the age of 50, but that's just a number. Being over 50 is a mindset. I have daily reminders that I am aging. There are the daily physical reminders, but as I reach middle age, I recognize that my priorities are changing. My family is growing up. Grandchildren remind me that there is a circle of life. Career aspirations change and retirement looms ahead.

Honestly, I'm tired. There may be other baby boomers who are invigorated, just like the ads I see on TV, but deep down inside, I think it's a front. I wish I could go back in time, as I evoke memories of my youth. I feel that I am on the edge to being beyond the middle age curve. Priorities can change overnight. Suddenly children are young adults and have moved out of the house. My parents are aging, and I see a role reversal, where I am now their caregiver.

Life is often stressful and frightening. My basic survival is front and center. Once upon a time, I imagined enjoyment of later years in my life as I got closer to retirement. But the realities of health, finances, and relationships are a jolting reminder that it's not all happy news. I have come to terms with my reality. I am aging, and there is no turning back the clock.

11. BUSINESS 8 TO 5

By day, I take on a different persona from that of my personal life. It's all about business. I work in an office. I have people around me all day long. I have a boss and co-workers. It's not necessarily how I would choose to live my time Monday through Friday from 8 to 5, but it's what I do to make a living.

Sometimes I am tasked with making decisions that involve purchasing products for my company. I'm not always the final person to make the decision, but I will have input on it. The money is not my own. And my job can be on the line for how I spend the company's money. So I need to make smart decisions that will help improve the profitability of my organization.

Deep down, I am most concerned about my job security. So for that reason, I am very protective and thoughtful when it comes to spending the company's money.

12. DID I MATTER?

I have found my purpose in life, and I want to leave a legacy that fulfills that purpose. I continually work toward fulfilling my mission while I'm alive. I would like to see my legacy remembered now, while I can see how my money is put to good use, as well as after I'm gone.

I make decisions about what organizations I contribute to based on the alignment of their passion and purpose with my own. I'm not an overly wealthy individual, but I have financial resources that enable me to leave a legacy.

I want my family to enjoy money that I have worked to earn, but I also want to share it beyond my family. I would like something that furthers a part of my life story. It would be affirming to know that my money is being used now and then after I'm gone for something positive. I feel an enormous sense of pride and goodwill, knowing that my money is being used for a good cause.

Now let's turn to how you can stimulate emotion.

CHAPTER 5

STIMULATE EMOTION

Attention span is the amount of concentrated time on a task without becoming distracted. You only have a few seconds to stimulate an individual's attention.

EIGHT SECONDS TO POUNCE

Eight seconds is the average attention span of today's reader,[11] with those precious seconds representing about the time to ready only 30 to 40 words of copy. Or about HERE (at 35 words). As recently as in 2000, the average attention span was 12 seconds. But when online and mobile use exploded, along with distractions from multiple streams of media, another one-third of our attention span was lopped off.

Those eight seconds only allow reading 30 to 40 words (based on my informal findings). That represents about 5 to 8 words for a headline followed by a couple of average length sentences, or three or four short sentences. That's all the time you've got to engage your reader to convince them to give you more time.

Consider these stats:

- Average attention span in 2015: 8.25 seconds
- Average attention span in 2000: 12.00 seconds

41

- Average number of times per hour an office worker checks their email box: 30
- Average length watched of a single internet video: 2.7 minutes

There are a few other stats out there that underscore how we, as a culture, don't pay attention for very long before moving on:

- Percent of web page views that last less than 4 seconds: 17%
- Percent of web page views that lasted more than 10 minutes: 4%
- Percent of words read on web pages with 111 words or less: 49%
- Percent of words read on an average (593 words) web page: 28%

There's more: users spend only 4.4 seconds more for each additional 100 words speed reading through web copy.

If you hope to stimulate emotion, your copy must quickly get to the point to interest the reader longer than a mere eight seconds.

THE RETICULAR ACTIVATING SYSTEM

Imagine how your message enters your prospect's mind where it zips past radar. The radar detector in the brain's processing pathway is called the Reticular Activating System (RAS). The RAS acts as a filter that determines what message goes to your conscious or subconscious mind.

The RAS filters the incoming information. Unknown to you, it commands what you pay attention to, influences how aroused you are, and filters what isn't going to get access deeper in your mind. Besides alerting the brain of environmental changes, the RAS also sends signals involving:

- Physical needs, such as hunger or thirst.
- Self-made choice, such as buying an object and then seeing it everywhere.
- Your name.
- Emotion.
- Contrast.
- New stimuli.

Before messages gain entry to your higher, thinking mind, the RAS assesses the input. If there are stress and negative emotions, you react instinctively and the "reactive mind" processes and sends the data right to the amygdala—the intuitive part of the brain that reacts in "fight or flight" mode. But if your mind is calm and there is relevance in the message, it goes further into the mind for processing. The RAS operates outside of your awareness. Another way to look at the RAS: it's the gatekeeper that your message first encounters. If the message is logical and sequential, the attention of the user will hold and allow you to communicate your key points and conclusion. Content constantly bombards your audience. The RAS works to filter out stimuli viewed as unimportant in an effort to prevent sensory overload. If something important (relevant, dangerous, interesting) presents itself, the RAS radar allows the sensory information (tactile, auditory, and visual) through for actual processing.

For example, if you're enjoying a cup of coffee, and someone comes from behind you and touches your shoulder, the RAS bumps that sensory information up and routes it to a decision-making part of the brain to take priority over the coffee you were enjoying.

Here's another example. In a noisy room at a party, or even a crowded boarding area at an airport, when your name is called you immediately hear it over everything else. That's the RAS alerting you to the information, and everything else will fall away from your attention.

So even if you intently focus on a visual activity, your RAS will allow relevant data from touch or sound to interrupt you when it's relevant to survival or safety, or otherwise somehow important to you.

The RAS also responds to uniqueness. It helps you notice anything new and different. Remember, it is your instinctive radar.

So, to challenge your thinking, which pathway ("reactive mind" or "thinking mind") do you want your message to be sent? Let's acknowledge that when you expose your prospect to your marketing messaging, your prospect's mind is going to be in a thinking place that's out of your control.

I think it depends on the environment, approach, and circumstance of your prospect. And even more important, it depends if you've first created the persona of your customer. You must fully internalize the persona of the individual you're trying to reach and customize your message for relevancy for a better chance of filtering your message to the "thinking mind." The action you desire (that is, how to stimulate attention) is more apt to come from the "thinking mind" than from the "reactive mind." But what if you can succeed at stimulating attention from the "reactive mind" first, so you have your prospect's full, undivided concentration?

The amygdala is on high alert when you experience negative emotions like fear, uncertainty, or doubt. Physiologically, when this happens, the brain absorbs available nutrients and oxygen and you go into survival mode. No new information can possibly get in. Your brain is stressed.

So to get further inside the brain, you must moderate the mood, or better, restore a positive mood. Once you calm and focus the brain, the amygdala opens the gate to send information to the prefrontal cortex, or the "thinking mind," to store memory.

Turn around the mood, and guess what happens? The amygdala rewards the mind with a neurochemical that strengthens the staying power of information presented. People remember more when they in a positive emotional state.

When the mood moderates, the information passes along to the hippocampus. Here the mind merges new sensory information with past memories and knowledge. These are "relational memories" (a good thing). When the mind focuses in a positive state, then "executive functions" take over. These functions (mentioned earlier) include:

- Judgment
- Analysis
- Organizing
- Problem solving
- Planning
- Creativity

With those "executive functions," the mind can turn memories into long-term knowledge.

The RAS is always on and screening incoming sensory data. It can work for you, or against you. You would be overwhelmed if you had to process everything that's coming at you right now. Most of that sensory data you're bombarded with every hour are not relevant or important. The RAS enables permission (and relief!) to "ignore" most of it.

Stimulate it appropriately, and you now have your prospect's undivided attention.

THE SPELL OF FOMO

The RAS filter can be continually cycling and checking to make sure you aren't left out of something important to you. That fear of being out of the loop can explain a phenomenon called FOMO: The "Fear of Missing Out."

Perhaps you've heard of it. Perhaps this particular fear describes you or someone you know. FOMO is a phenomenon reported by 56 percent of social media users,[12] and it even has its own hashtag. This particular fear isn't just of missing out on social media posts; it extends to checking email, phone calls, and more. More importantly to marketers, the driving emotion of the FOMO is powerful, and when properly used, you can write copy and create messaging to leverage this basic human fear.

The term FOMO was added to the Oxford English Dictionary in 2013. The acronym may be new, but classically trained direct mail copywriters have recognized the power of the fear of missing out for generations. You can use it in your copy to effectively sell because of how the brain is wired.

With mobile technology today, it is possible to become genuinely addicted to social networks because of the fear of missing out. It's now effortless to compare and evaluate your own life with that of your friends.

A survey goes on to report:

- 51 percent visit or log on to social networking sites more frequently than two years earlier.
- The average person manages 3.1 email addresses (up from 2.6 a year earlier).
- 27 percent check their social networks as soon as they wake up.
- 42 percent have multiple social networking accounts (61 percent for those age 18 to 34).

- 56 percent are afraid of missing an event, news, or an important status update if they don't keep an eye on social networks.

These stats suggest you're more likely than not to be under the spell of FOMO. But the reality is this: The RAS and amygdala are coded to have instinctive fear. And without taking inappropriate advantage of your prospective customers, there are ways you can engage the RAS and amygdala that make your sales messaging more effective. Here are three ways you can use FOMO as you write copy and create message positioning:

- **First to Know.** If you fear missing out, you must surely want to be the first to know of an important development, new product, or news story. When you're the first to know, you're eager to tell others you're the first to know and share it (to your ego's benefit).
- **Inside Story.** People like to have the inside scoop combined with effective storytelling. Combine the concepts of revealing your inside story with a unique selling proposition, or positioning, to create synergy.
- **Limited Time.** When there is a limited time that a product is available, it intensifies desire to acquire it now. The challenge today, however, is that it's easy for customers to check out competition and discover that limited time appeal has its constraints.

These uses also create urgency in your copy. Writing copy and messaging based on this intense human primal fear will drive higher response. There can be no question that the spell of FOMO is real and a part of your customer's minds.

THE AMYGDALA: FIGHT OR FLIGHT

The amygdala, or lizard brain, has an evolutionary purpose for humans to survive and pass on genetic information through reproduction. The amygdala is reacts in a "fight" or "flight" mode. It regulates anger, fear, and sex, with memory formulated over a lifetime, as it assesses how to respond to survive and reproduce.

The right amygdala retains negative emotions, especially fear and sadness.

The left amygdala retains both pleasant and unpleasant emotions.

By understanding the personas of prospective customers or donors, you can better forecast the way they will respond so you can stimulate the mind, and importantly, anticipate the most likely way she or he will initially react.

It is important to understand the role of the amygdala as a part of brain function. How the amygdala is stimulated and calmed can influence a prospect's desire to buy.

When you stimulate your prospect's mind using fear, uncertainty, and doubt, you stimulate the most inner, fundamental human emotions of anger, safety, or desire for reproduction. Alternatively, positivity stimulates optimism to continue to engage with the message or join the conversation. But for the most part, it's negativity that is most effective, with the possible exception of using social media where positivity is effective.

On an individual level, fear is your greatest attention-getter. And let's clarify the distinction between fear and safety. Fear doesn't keep you safe; fear is a secondary response. The function of the amygdala is to assure your survival.

The amygdala is not associated with conscious thinking. When you ponder something in the future and you become afraid, this is not a fight/flight response because you're not in imminent danger. It is something fabricated in your head, which hasn't happened in the past and is not happening in the moment.

The amygdala works to ensure your survival. It kicks in only because it senses immediate danger or threat. And when it activates, the rest of your brain is put on temporary hold. You don't have time to be afraid. You don't have time to think. You either flee or fight before fear begins. It's automatic.

Fear is an emotion that comes after the fight or flight response. Fear by itself is not useful as a protection mechanism. Awareness of a situation is useful, but does not imply fear.

Fear is not real. It exists in your thoughts of the future. It's a creation of your mind. Danger is real, but fear is not.

This distinction is important for marketers to understand. This distinction is leverage you can use to make your messaging more impactful. As the advertising saying goes, "perception is reality." But no matter the reality, if fear is your perception, fear is in your mind, and is your reality.

CONDITIONED TO FEAR

While fear is instinctive, you can argue it's also a conditioned response that influences your day-to-day lives. For example, you hear praise for good behavior, but are punished for poor behavior (even when poor behavior is unintentional).

Think about when you said something and you were laughed at by your peers. It embarrassed you, and you learned to be afraid of that embarrassment. It happens again and again, because you're human and occasionally things come out of your mouth before you have time to think. Too many instances of opening your mouth prematurely and embarrassing yourself conditions you to keep your mouth shut.

Even if most conditioning happens early in life, some still occurs as an adult. For example, you may have developed a fear of the police after speeding and getting a ticket. In another scenario, you were not careful with what you said and got in an argument. Now you never fight back.

If you did something for which you were punished, and that situation is repeated a few more times, the punishment is reinforced, so you're now conditioned to be afraid of similar future situations.

Everybody is afraid of something. Fear is exacerbated by many tasks, such as reading or watching the news. Or, if it's political advertising season (as it seems to be almost continuously), you can be overwhelmed with negative messaging.

Fear is constantly in front of us, not only on the news, but also in entertainment. Whether it's dark television shows or movies, you can't escape fear in mass media.

When your mind is in persistent fear, you cannot think any longer. You're stuck. You're insecure. You're lacking basic self-esteem and self-confidence. You cannot make up your mind. Your decision-making power is blocked. That's why marketers must, at one level, leverage the power of fear and emotional stimulation. However, you must quickly move to calm the mind so that decision-making is unblocked and you can move your customer to the thinking part of their brain.

STIMULATING EMOTION WITH TASTY WORDS AND LANGUAGE

Taste-related words and figurative language can stimulate and be more deliciously persuasive and sumptuously effective than literal words with the same meaning.

Words that stimulate taste-activated areas in the brain are known to be associated with emotional processing. Language that frequently uses physical sensations or objects that refer to abstract domains, such as time, understanding, or emotion, actually requires more brainpower, resulting in more engagement and comprehension.

To illustrate the point, the sentence, "She looked at him sweetly," sparks more brain activity in emotion-based regions, like the amygdala, than "She looked at him kindly." Why? Because "sweet" amplifies a more physical experience, according to research from Princeton University and the Free University of Berlin.[13] Figurative language can be more persuasive and effective in copywriting because your message is more imaginable in the reader's mind.

For copy and messaging, when practical (and without going overboard), a few tasty, figurative words can stimulate a more emotional reaction from your prospective customers. Figurative language works because the copy goes beyond the actual meanings of words. This way, the reader gains new insights into the objects or subjects in the message. Here are seven types of figurative language to consider using in copy and messaging.

1. **Simile**. A simile compares two things using the words "like" and "as." Examples include:
   a. Clean as a whistle.
   b. Brave as a lion.
   c. Stand out like a sore thumb.
2. **Metaphor.** When you use a metaphor, you make a statement that doesn't make literal sense, like "time is a thief." It only makes sense when the similarities between the two things become apparent or someone understands the connection. Examples include:
   a. Time is money.
   b. He has a heart of stone.
   c. America is a melting pot.
3. **Personification.** When you give human characteristics to inanimate objects, animals or ideas, this is personification. This can affect the way your customer imagines things. Examples include:

    a.   Opportunity knocked on the door.

    b.   The sun can greet you tomorrow morning.

    c.   The sky was full of dancing stars.

4. **Hyperbole.** Hyperbole is an outrageous exaggeration that emphasizes a point, and can be ridiculous or funny. Hyperbole is useful in fiction to add color, but should be used sparingly and with caution in marketing copy. Examples are:

    a.   You snore louder than a freight train.

    b.   It's a small town. I spent a couple of weeks there one day.

    c.   You could have knocked me over with a feather.

5. **Symbolism.** Symbolism occurs when a word has meaning in itself, but it's used to represent something entirely different. In this case, work with your graphics team, as images can powerfully express symbolism powerfully. Examples are:

    a.   Using an image of a flag to represent patriotism and a love for one's country.

    b.   Using an apple pie to represent an American lifestyle.

    c.   Using an apple to represent education.

6. **Alliteration.** Alliteration is a repetition of the first consonant sounds in several words. An example:

    a.   Wide-eyed and wondering while we wait for the other ones to waken.

7. **Onomatopoeia.** Onomatopoeia is the use of words that sound like their meaning. They add a level of fun and reality to writing. Here are some examples:

    a.   The burning wood hissed and crackled.

    b.   Words that sound like their meaning include: beep, boom, bong, clang, click, crunch, gobble, hum, meow, munch, oink, pow, quack, smash, swish, tweet, wham, whoosh, zap and zing.

Figurative language can stimulate emotion and enable people to visualize your product or service more instinctively. With tasty copy, you heighten senses that immerse prospects and customers to more powerfully open themselves to the possibility of possessing what you have to offer.

STIMULATING THE 12 PERSONAS

With the perspective about the amygdala and how humans respond, it's time to revisit the 12 personas laid out earlier, and consider how you can stimulate emotion from this type of individual.

1. Trailblazers/Early Adopters

I fear being left behind and missing out on the latest and newest. My emotional fears are stoked when I'm not the first to know. I read, watch videos and am up-to-date in what's new. I also research information to check out if something is real or a hoax. This is a mental competition to me. I must stay current because I don't want to ever feel behind-the-curve and slip on the Diffusion of Innovations curve from being an "Innovator" to an "Early Adopter." I would just die if I slipped even farther to the boring and unimaginative "Early Majority." My peers would recognize my downfall, and that could be the end of my status as a leading-edge "Innovator."

2. My Brand/My Lifestyle/My Growth

I am highly protective of my brand. I constantly fear my brand and my status will be lost. As a result, I am constantly grooming myself, both literally and figuratively, so that I have an edge in my career and personal life. Maintaining that level of personal brand requires ongoing attention and I'm always on guard about protecting my brand. I fear my lifestyle will come under threat. I fear that I won't be seen at the right place or that I'm not growing intellectually.

I fear being left behind and that my personal brand will suffer. I fear that I will not stand apart from the crowd and that I will blend in and be merely average.

- My appearance is a personal brand in a trademark.
- My appearance must support my lifestyle.

- I wouldn't be caught underdressed or not looking right when in public.
- I'm not afraid to stand apart from the crowd.
- If my appearance isn't just right, I fear suffering the consequences to my personal brand.
- I fear my lifestyle could vanish.
- I fear I won't keep up with personal growth opportunities so I am on constant alert.

Some days I'm a fashionista. Professionally I may be a sales representative. I am highly engaged in personal development and go to seminars, read, and enjoy networking.

3. Money Matters

I fear waste. I fear being sucked into situations that threatens my pragmatism. I don't want to be walked down a primrose path that leads to wasted time and money. And I certainly don't want to be seen as unnecessarily extravagant.

As I review marketing materials, I fear that a product may not support who I am or my values. I fear overpaying. I especially fear I have overpaid on something I have recently purchased. Seeing a sale after I have made a purchase puts me off. I don't want stability in my life to be rocked.

- I'm naturally skeptical of all claims.
- I fear being misled and ripped off and being betrayed by anyone or any organization that I do business with.
- I fear my hard-earned money will be wasted.
- I fear I will be taken advantage of.

Because of my fears, I am less apt to make quick decisions. I can quickly have buyer's remorse about any buying decision that I make. When I am reminded of my fears, I seek information that will help reassure me and calm my mind.

4. On Financial Edge

I fear that someday I'm not going to have the money to pay for basic items like food. I can't afford good nutritious food, so I get what's available and fast.

Earning enough money is an ongoing struggle and money problems are constantly on my mind. Sometimes I use a bank as a place to keep my money. But a lot of times I simply look for alternative ways to keep my money. I like credit cards. Sometimes I have to get a short-term payday loan. My emotion is stimulated when I see a place that will give me a credit lifeline. But all too often I'm unable to charge any more on a credit card—that's if I even have one that I can use. So I have to look for alternatives.

Because of the difficulty for me to understand how to manage money, I sometimes feel threatened and intimidated by all of the fine print of credit offers.

Living day-to-day, sometimes I wake up in the morning not knowing how I'm going to get through the week. The next pay day can't come fast enough. Sometimes I wonder if I'm going to have a place to live. I'm especially concerned about losing my car. Without a car, I can't get to work. If I have to choose what to pay first, I'll pay for my car over other things. I can always sleep in my car for a few nights if needed. A lot of people around me don't know what I'm dealing with deep inside.

5. Right Thing to Do: Taking the High Road

I fear my moral compass will be compromised. I am shaken when things go wrong. It is unnerving to me when I see others being taken advantage of, and when our culture and society take directional turns away from what our belief systems and foundational principles should be. I'm a bit negative about the world around me, and to a degree I look down on others who don't live up to certain standards.

My fears include:

- If the right things aren't supported, the world and our culture will spiral downward.
- People around me aren't doing their part.

- The world is ending up in a worse state than how it was given to me.
- Fear of regretting that I didn't do more to make the world a better place.

I believe that issues such as climate change are huge, and needs to be addressed now, at any cost. I want to choose automobiles that are the most environmentally friendly. It's the right thing to do!

6. Love and Social Relationships

With my basic need to have people close to me, my fear is that a purchase decision will make people look down on me. I have a strong fear that anything can jeopardize a relationship. I need affirmation from friends. I fear missing out. Some days I find myself living on social media as I clamor for attention and affirmation. My fears include:

- I won't be loved.
- A relationship could falter.
- Being disliked, discredited, or rejected.
- That my "street cred" will be diminished and social ranking negatively impacted

I fear being left out of social plans made by other people. I don't need to be the center of attention. I'm perfectly happy to be on the sidelines. It would hurt me tremendously if I were not included with friends and if I were banished from any social activities.

7. Adrenaline Seekers: Opportunists

I fear missing big opportunities. I fear being left out of the action when I can seize an opportunity. It's often fueled by the opportunity to make or to win money. I fear the establishment, and for that reason, I like to seek out my own path.

Here's what I believe:

- I think the odds are stacked against me.
- I fear for missed opportunities that may never come back again, so I seize them.
- No one has my back, so I believe I have to make a mark on the world on my own.

I want to believe I can beat the house or beat the system. The psychological lift of winning trumps the dollars. I don't like to follow the establishment. I seek hidden opportunities to make money.

8. Safe Players

I fear risk. I abhor it. I fear risking everything imaginable: losing money, failing health, breaking relationships, and much more. I'm often on edge, so it's easy to stimulate my emotions. As I read information and do my research, I am easily scared away by marketing and selling messages. My emotions and fears include:

- Making a decision that will cost me dearly.
- Living in doubt so my self-confidence is low.
- Risky situations that stimulate my emotions and fears.

I can be repelled quickly from an organization's sales message if it doesn't include safety. I admit that I am highly frugal. I'm different from other people who seek value. For example, I'm a person who likes to have maximum coverages for insurance. I like safety systems. With the future seemingly uncertain, I don't rest easily at night.

9. Hiding My Compulsion

I fear being found out. Hiding my compulsion is of utmost importance and highly influences my decisions that I make. I see my secret compulsion as a weakness. I was bullied as a child because other kids could see through me at the time when I felt most vulnerable. Childhood experiences have grooved deep memories for me that can never be changed. I fear that no one empathizes with my situation. I fear being ostracized. I fear that the life I have now, as imperfect as it is, could be forever changed in a very bad way with just one misstep. For that reason:

- I fear my compulsions will somehow be exposed for everyone to see.
- I'm always on my guard.
- I continually compensate to cover-up my insecurities.

I fear I will never be normal or even just average. I see myself as an outlier. I prefer to move away from the mainstream. I hope the people around me think of me as normal, but I'm afraid that the perception of me by other people can change in a heartbeat. I see a chink in my armor, and hope that people around me don't perceive my weakness.

10. Fifty Plus

I fear that I won't get to live the happy, carefree life that I see on display in advertising. I fear my health will decline. I fear I haven't saved enough money to retire. I fear and have seen other people experience age discrimination in culture, as well as workplaces that marginalizes older workers.

The circle of life has changed. I'm on a different side of the circle, where it's me, a formidable baby boomer, who is being replaced. Technology changes so rapidly, and it's hard for me to keep up. I didn't get to enjoy using a smartphone, texting, social media, or the Internet until middle age. I've adapted, but I'm weary of keeping up any longer.

I fear my youth and importance as a baby boomer in our culture is coming to an end. I sense the world is passing me by. This point in my life has fears that are becoming more magnified as I see an uncertain future.

11. Business 8 to 5

I feel pretty good about my job security, but there is always a fear of screwing up. It might not result in me being fired, but it can show up on a job review in the future. And can have negative lasting results for my ability to be promoted in the future.

In instances where I am unhappy with a current vendor, my emotion can be stimulated if I see a better approach that will improve my company's bottom line.

My emotion is also stimulated any time there is a possible threat to either my job security or how I will be viewed in the office. I'm very sensitive to any outcome concerning change.

12. Did I Matter?

I fear that the good things I have done in my life won't be completely recognized. I fear being forgotten after I am gone, and that my relevance will slowly dissipate. I fear that my skills will be less important. I want the skills that I have accumulated over my lifetime to be recognized and appreciated. I fear:

- My contributions to humanity will leave me largely unimportant in the world.
- My life is incomplete.
- Being forgotten by people important to me in my life now and in future generations.

After spending so much of my life in other endeavors, I've begun to realize that I don't want to be seen as irrelevant. As I reach the point of end-of-life planning, I can reduce my fears with generosity. And I don't want to be seen as someone who accumulated wealth and didn't share it. By giving, I can moderate my fear of being perceived as greedy.

Now let's turn to how you can calm the mind.

CHAPTER 6

CALM THE MIND

Persona

Stimulate

Calm

Stimulate. Calm. These are two related, but contrasting, messaging and copywriting concepts that marketers and copywriters should master. Why? Because stimulating emotion by leveraging the RAS filter and amygdala is a sure-fire way to get attention from prospective customers. But you don't want to drop the ball there. You must then immediately calm the mind so your prospects' fears are relieved. Encourage them to become engaged with your message so they will pause long enough for you to introduce them to your solution.

UNBLOCK DECISION MAKING

In the previous chapter, I described the Reticular Activating System (RAS). The RAS and the amygdala, where your fear is processed, are closely related. Fear paralyzes thinking because it's an instinctive response from the amygdala, the lizard brain.

Because fear is an overwhelming natural response, it, too, shuts off the thinking part of the brain. While you want to stimulate emotion tapping into fear, uncertainty, and doubt, you need to quickly calm the mind and let the amygdala cool down to unblock decision making. You can begin to calm the mind by presenting new information—a solution—for your audience to moderate their mood.

Search the Web for "how do you calm the mind" and you'll get thousands of websites with meditation advice. While you don't

Position

Story

Interpret

Permission

59

want to steer prospects to meditate—at least in the stereotypical way you think of meditation—you do want your prospect to be calmed enough to focus on your message.

AFFIRMATIONS

A big obstacle is that people are not always open with giving other people positive affirmations. There is a tremendous amount of negativity out there. As you'll learn shortly, there is a reason why. Though people's brains are physically "wired" to respond to negativity, people also gravitate toward positivity. You see this in mainstream media and in social media. While there are negative headlines, there is usually an effort made to disseminate positive news as part of the complete package of information. Social media has also played a part in this shift. The most shared and commented-on posts tend to be positive, feel-good news. Social media can be calming.

The challenge for marketers is to help prospective customers decide for themselves that they, the customer, can be positive. That is done through affirmations, and it's easier to do than you might expect. You simply have to shift your mindset from the negative to the positive.

For the positive to be successful, you need to acknowledge and relate to people's fears, uncertainties, and doubts in life. Once you have expressed that you are conscious of these fears, uncertainties, and doubts, you are in a much better position to have earned the trust of your reader.

Stimulation of the amygdala can trigger intense emotions, such as aggression or fear. In its extreme, it can cause a panic attack.

It's the voice of fear, uncertainty, and doubt that you often hear loudest. This is the "gut reaction," or those subjective feelings you experience.

The amygdala is also where memory and emotions are combined. When the reward is pleasing, the behavior and association may last a lifetime. Likewise, the suffering and embarrassment of punishment may be remembered for a long time too.

For instance, if a sound in the external world occurs right before something painful happens, you associate that sound with the painful event, and that sound will then later trigger a protective defense response. But, if the sound occurs just before eating when you're hungry, then the sound will be associated with that kind of positive event.

The amygdala is forming associations between random or neutral external stimuli and events—both positive and negative—that will embed those experiences in a stronger, lifelong way.

This concept is substantiated in the famous classical conditioning study by Ivan Pavlov.[14] Pavlov and his assistants experimented with dogs that had surgically implanted tubes in their saliva glands. They presented the dogs with meat powder, and subsequently had their saliva collected. After a period of time, they noticed that dogs began salivating before the meat powder was presented, whether this was from the presence of the experimenter in the lab coat or the bell ringing. This discovery meant that salivation was not due to an automatic process, but was a learned response.

To quote Robert Sylwester in *A Celebration of Neurons*, "Emotion drives attention which drives learning."[15] When you make people feel something, they not only pay attention to the message, but also tend to remember it.

Marketers can influence how a product or organization calms an individual's mind by merely seeing a logo and brand colors, category of product, or your organization's name. Your challenge as a marketer is how to stimulate emotion in the amygdala, then calm it down and give it enough satisfaction so the brain thinks that it's taking in stimuli that will satisfy those basic human instincts.

Your brain is primarily interested in two things: first, surviving what's potentially dangerous, and second, doing what's pleasurable.

For instance, if you just now heard a loud crash, a scream, smelled smoke, or someone startled you while reading this book, you'd jump and lose complete connection with this written message. Why? Because your brain sensed danger. Your primitive brain function is also motivated by eating and sex. It's no accident that messages around food and sex work in advertising.

The amygdala is a powerful distractor of your train of thought. And if it happens to you, it happens to your prospective customer. For example, you want to be thin and you say you'll exercise and eat healthier, but you don't. Why? One reason may be that the amygdala survival instinct prevails by telling you that you need more food now because it may be awhile before you can eat again.

Here's another example. You know you have a deadline to write that marketing plan, or sales letter, or maybe clean the kitchen before guests arrive. However, the pleasure instinct patterns of the amygdala derails you and you decide to check Facebook first because doing that gives you greater pleasure.

Just as the amygdala puts food and Facebook before other priorities in your mind, it's doing the same to your customers and prospects. So the opportunity for you, the marketer, is "How does your marketing message become as calming as food or Facebook?"

I believe that within the core of almost every product or service, you can create an emotional appeal to survival and pleasure.

5 APPEALS TO BASIC HUMAN PRIMAL INSTINCTS

Here are five hints about how you can appeal to basic human primal emotions and instincts.

1. **Engage Emotion First.** Logic can wait. How many successful marketing initiatives have you seen that hit someone over the head with logic, or an in-your-face offer? The most successful advertising, be it TV, video, print ads, a direct mail letter, email message, or content marketing, begins with emotion. Blame it on the amygdala, if you want. But like it or not, you—the marketer—are not going to change how the human brain processes your marketing message. So rather than resist human instinct of survival and pleasure, embrace it and appeal to an emotional level that's on par with, or exceeds, the instinct to get food or check Facebook.

2. **Create a Framework.** You might think about your message in three broad parts, beginning first with fear, uncertainty, and doubt. Calm the stress. Follow it with your unique selling proposition. Then reveal the solution. Pace your message with a framework in mind.

3. **Tell a Story.** Storytelling is an effective technique as you communicate your message. Think about any viral video your friends have shared with you, and in it, you'll see a video story that's entertaining, puts a smile on your face, tugs at your heartstrings, or delivers hope of some kind. Most

importantly, it gives you pure pleasure to watch, or the pleasure to know that you can make a difference.

4. **Be Clear.** Don't bore. Your prospective customers see boring stuff all the time that's confusing, inarticulate and overly detailed. Some marketers overreact and, in a knee-jerk reaction, conclude that messaging must be short because people's attention spans are short. While it could be true that most of us, as consumers, have short attention spans, that isn't what derails the prospect from your message. It's that the marketing messaging doesn't stimulate the emotion, then calm the mind with your solution.

5. **Give Permission to Act.** This should be given to your audience through your marketing affirmation messaging so that they become customers. Today's consumer resistance to "being sold" is higher than ever, yet consumers want to buy when they're satisfied that their decision is right. You have to craft your message so prospective customers are given permission, affirmed, and want to buy. It may take more time to make the sale, and you may need to give more good reasons, but you must help your customer give themselves permission to buy. Engage them through story, educate them through logic, and build anticipation so they have a desire to convert themselves to being your customer.

These five ideas are meant to appeal to the most basic of human primal emotions. To better grasp the connection between stimulating emotion and the need to calm the mind, it may be helpful to take a deeper dive into how our brains respond to stimuli. Your brain is filled with neurotransmitters. Knowing the signals they transmit will help you better understand how the brain functions. For marketers, it's important that you know how to use these signals to strengthen your messaging.

Neurotransmitters are the brain chemicals that transfer information throughout your brain and body. They transmit signals between nerve cells, called "neurons." While this was mentioned earlier, it's worth repeating: The brain uses neurotransmitters to tell your heart to beat, your lungs to breathe, and your stomach to digest. They can also affect mood, sleep, concentration, and weight, and can cause adverse symptoms when they are out of balance.

A COCKTAIL OF BRAIN CHEMICALS

There are two kinds of neurotransmitters: inhibitory and excitatory. Excitatory neurotransmitters stimulate the brain. Inhibitory neurotransmitters calm the brain and help create stability.

So after stimulating emotion, you must quickly balance the mood. When you over-stimulate, the inhibitory neurotransmitters can be depleted. Instead of focusing on your solution, you leave your prospect focusing on their fear, uncertainty, and doubt.

Those inhibitory neurotransmitters—those brain chemicals—include:

- Serotonin, which is necessary for an even mood.
- Gaba, which helps to calm and relax us by balancing stimulation over-firing.
- Dopamine, which is a special neurotransmitter because it is considered to be both excitatory and inhibitory. When it spikes, it can motivate and give a person pleasure. When elevated or low, it can cause focus issues such as forgetting what a paragraph said when you just finished reading it (obviously, not something marketers want to have happen).

With a cocktail of brain chemicals swirling around in your prospect's mind, here are a few ways you can calm it after stimulating his or her emotion:

- Announce a new discovery.
- Introduce a solution.
- Assure with a promise.
- Promise a reward.
- Brighten the mood of the message to evoke pleasant memory.
- Introduce new learning.

CALM THE MIND WITH THESE EMOTIONS

Scientists used to recognize six classic emotions:

- Happy
- Surprised
- Afraid
- Disgusted
- Angry
- Sad

However, after a study at the University of Glasgow,[16] scientists discovered that anger and disgust have the same facial expressions, as do fear and surprise. However, in the long term, the face did show distinction in the two, meaning that this distinction is socially, not biologically, based.

How does this apply to marketers? After you have taken the prospect to fear, you need to take them to another emotion. While it could be suggested that calming the mind means bringing your prospect to a happy place, in reality, calming the mind can also take someone to sadness, anger, and disgust, further explained below. What's important is that you have stimulated your prospect's undivided attention and you move them to an emotional place where you control the message. Manage the response to your message, and you have a better chance of controlling the outcome.

Sadness is an emotion that helps your prospect connect and empathize. Research says that when you experience sadness, your brain releases a stress hormone called cortisol, along with a hormone that promotes connection and empathy called oxytocin. This makes you more generous and trusting. Taken a step further, fundraising research has found that people whose brain releases oxytocin are also more likely to give money to others. Watch a video titled Empathy, Neurochemistry, and the Dramatic Arc[17] at CustomerMindCode.com/Resources.

Anger and disgust bring out different responses, such as stubbornness. Rude comments on blog posts make people dig in deeper about their stance, either in agreement or disagreement. But if comments were civil, people had no change of opinion. Provoke anger and disgust, and you encourage engagement in your message.

Then there is happiness. Happiness makes you want to share, and joy can be a driver of response. In social media, it's happiness that is the main driver for sharing. If you want your content to be virally shared, the top ten emotions (studied by Fractl)[18] include:

- Amusement
- Interest
- Surprise
- Happiness
- Delight
- Pleasure
- Joy
- Hope
- Affection
- Excitement

Other studies suggest that positive content is more likely to go viral than negative content.[19] And consider this: When your prospect shares, likes, or comments, it's a gift being sent back to the sender. It's the reciprocal energy of positive giving that makes your prospect's energy higher, and when that happens, it also affirms the creator of the content.

Positive words mean things. So do sounds. If you're a casual listener of music you may not have considered how the key that music is written in influences your mood.

7 FEELINGS THAT ADD WARMTH AND CALM

Sometimes you get too close to the bells and whistles of your product and service. When that happens, it can be helpful to step back and remember what is near and dear to the heart of your prospective customer. Push away bright-shiny features and techno-speak, and ask yourself if any of these "7 Feelings" can open a new pathway for you to be invited inside your prospect's mind.

As a marketer, you know there are many ways to persuade someone to read or listen to your sales message, such as money, success, respect, and influence.

But perhaps you need an emotional hook. With simplicity and emotion in mind, here are "7 Feelings" where you can bring warmth and emotion to your copy and message.

1. **Family.** What more important value can there be than the love a person has for family. Family-centered safety and warmth is a winner about every time it's used. When most people think about what's most important in their lives, it's family.

2. **Friends.** Including friends into a sales message can free up the mind from the drudgery of day-to-day work. Most people associate friends with entertainment, time together, and sharing of personal relationships.

3. **Fun.** With people's senses so often bombarded with negative news, a fun or playful spirit in your sales message can lighten the mental load. Most people would rather play than work. Fun invites involvement. Involvement invites response.

4. **Food.** This tasty four-letter F-word gets your attention, doesn't it? Now that you've read it, you might be salivating. Just the word "food" can trigger basic human desire to eat. That snack or dessert you're imagining tastes yummy, doesn't it?

5. **Fashion.** Deep down, you want to look good. Clothes and fashion help create a personal branding statement. Most people want to be attractive, and most people are attracted to others who look good.

6. **Fitness.** People have good intentions about being fit and healthy, even if they don't want to hit the gym and know they could do better. So, get attention by conveying how you can contribute to someone's improved health.

7. **Fido/Felines.** When was the last time you watched a video on social media featuring a cat or dog? You can admit it. You do it. So you can

hardly go wrong when you introduce a lovable or quirky pet into your marketing message.

Simple emotions? Yes. Sometimes a little nudge is needed to remind you it's the small things that calm people's feelings.

COLORS THAT STIMULATE AND CALM

There is growing scientific evidence of how the brain processes color and how color impacts your feelings and responses. Over the years, some marketers have wondered about color's contribution to the overall success of marketing. However, color usually isn't high on the list of test priorities. Unless you have great flexibility to test colors, most marketers simply go with the colors they feel will work best.

From experience, I know that direct mail outer envelopes with vivid colors, such as the fruitcake example noted previously that featured a wood grain look, grab attention. The response rate increase over a plain white envelope proves the point. Colors that correspond with the desired feel of financial services (light blue and marbling effects) are proven to increase response.

If you're unsure of the color to use, you don't have to go with your gut, considering what research tells us.

Here I'll share with you recent research from university studies, along with *The Theory of Colours* by Johann Wolfgang von Goethe,[20] first published in 1810. Goethe created one of the first color wheels and shared psychological impact. His theories are still widely adopted:

- Red conveys gravity and dignity.
- Yellow connotes brightness and soft excitement, yet noble.
- Blue is at odds with itself, being both exciting and retreating.
- Green is reassuring.

So how do these 200-year-old conclusions stack up against recent research that expands into more colors? A 2014 study of logos by the University of Missouri-Columbia[21] suggests additional consideration:

- Blue logos invoke feelings of confidence, success and reliability.
- Green logos invoke perceptions of environmental friendliness, toughness, durability, masculinity and sustainability.
- Purple logos invoke femininity, glamor and charm.
- Pink logos give the perception of youth, imagination and fashion.
- Yellow logos invoke perceptions of fun and modernity.
- Red logos brought feelings of expertise and self-assurance.

Other recent studies from the University of British Columbia[22] and Dartmouth College[23] make these observations:

- People have emotional responses to color. Those responses are linked to the brain's neural processes.
- The brain is most triggered by red, then green, then blue.
- Red can make people's work more accurate. Blue can make people more creative.
- People tested with red, blue or neutral backgrounds on computer screens found red to be more effective for recall and attention to detail. Blue was better for creating imagination.
- If you seek "avoidance" action (for example, toothpaste for cavity prevention), studies show red to have greater appeal. Conversely, if you seek "positive" action (for example, "tooth whitening"), then blue holds more appeal.
- Across cultures, red represents "no." It's a common emotional association that is innate. A study involving monkeys (a species that doesn't process the meaning of a red stop sign) found that the animals avoided humans who wore red.
- Red is also credited with helping people focus.
- Red is a color of stimulation.
- Blue is more relaxing and calming.

Remember, though, when considering colors: You must consider context. The visual impact of words or images in isolated environments can be different than when you are trying to connect a user to a brand, website, or direct mail package. For example, on the outer envelope of a direct mail package, my experience has found that a specific shade of blue, used with pin stripes and a marbling effect, increases response for financial products. Why? Likely it's because blue is calming, and the combination of pin stripes and marbling look formal and official.

Bottom line: As you prepare your next direct mail package, print ad, email HTML, website, landing pages, or video background, consider your environment and desired reaction from your prospective customers.

CALMING THE 12 PERSONAS

Let's return to the 12 personas and consider ideas about how you can calm their mind:

1. Trailblazers/Early Adopters

When I experience calm, it's because I'm surrounded by the latest and greatest. I feel like a kid in a candy store. I'm confident when I have access to new products before they are ever made available to the world. I'm a sucker for getting the inside scoop, especially when the inside skinny is for me and only a few select people.

I'm smart and savvy. When companies deliver information and feed my ego, I reward them with loyalty and social following.

When my mind is calmed, I'm open to engagement. Convince me, and I'll be a loyal follower and evangelist.

2. My Brand/My Lifestyle/My Growth

I am at my calmest when I know that my brand, lifestyle, and growth are being supported. You can calm my mind by feeding my ego and telling me that I have a good appearance, or you can feed my ego with positivity. I like things that are aesthetically pleasing. I like to feel I will learn something just by reading your sales message. I want to know that I can achieve more. When there is the promise that I will learn something or be inspired in any message, I am engaged.

Praise and compliments will reinforce that I am fulfilling my personal brand strategy. I want to be assured that my personal brand will be advanced whenever I am seen with a product.

I yearn for words of affirmation. Design must be up-to-date and evolve with the times.

My head will swell with pride and I'll feel like a million dollars when I receive praise from people around me, whether it's because of my appearance or my knowledge.

I am quickly and easily calmed. But if you don't calm my sensitive personality and emotion early on in our conversation, you will lose me.

3. Money Matters

Calm my mind with the promise there will be value and a marketer's message won't be a waste of my time. But the message must be genuine, without overdoing it. I'm naturally more skeptical than most. Too much flare and you can quickly turn me off. I will see through any over-hype of a marketing message. It must be sincere. Sincerity and steadiness will calm my mind.

- I must be assured I'm getting value.
- I need access to data, so I can conduct my own research.
- Give me an initial illustration how the product is a good value with charts, graphs, or numbers.
- Testimonials, early on, from people like me adds affirmation.
- Make me feel more secure than I will with competitors.

I'm naturally apprehensive and hesitate about parting with my hard-earned money. I consider myself stable and I don't want that aspect of my life disrupted. I must be assured that a marketer isn't wasting my time. When a marketer demonstrates how they have my best interests at heart, I'll reward them with my business.

4. On Financial Edge

I am most calm when I can see a pathway ahead of me where I won't be short on cash. When I know I can find a place to live that will accept my situation and late rent payment, I'm temporarily calmed. I would be calmed if I knew that my car was not going to a pose a problem for me. Knowing I can provide for my family also calms me.

I hope to be able to work with people and companies who can empathize and appreciate my situation. Being able to trust someone and an organization would be helpful in my life. When I see someone like me who needs a hand, I do what I can to help them. Especially family. I know that someday I'm going to need help, too.

Life is a struggle. And I do my best to put on a positive face. But if I can just see a chance to get ahead, I will feel much better about myself. I just need a break.

5. Right Thing to Do: Taking the High Road

I am at peace with people and organizations who share the same journey, path and values that I do. I simply cannot accept mediocrity. I want to see exacting standards. This is how my emotion is calmed. I want to see that an organization is going the extra mile and that their commitment is to leave the world a better place.

Here are other ways that my mind is calmed:

- When a decision supports my deep values, the price doesn't matter.
- I feel good about myself and my beliefs when a product supports my point of view.
- I want to be assured that the world will be a better place because of an organization's commitment, and that they are on my side.
- I want to see how my decisions will help support a more sustainable world.

I am loyal to any organization once I can trust it. I need to be shown how that organization will make the world a better place. I want them to reciprocate with their loyalty and commitment to my belief system. I will reward them with my business. When it's demonstrated to me that an organization has started a movement to bring more people to my way of thinking, that's an added bonus and oftentimes a decision tipping point.

6. Love and Social Relationships

When all is well in my life I am calm. When things are out of balance in my life and are not going well I will be distracted and stressed. So I need to be calmed through empathy. To me it's less about the promise of what your product or service will ultimately do for me, but how a company opens up to me and listens to me. I need to have time invested in me from an organization to calm my mind. But once I feel that I am being listened to I am more receptive to a message. These are a few ways that I can be calmed:

- I need to feel that my friends and family will agree with me because I have followed an organization or I purchase a specific product.
- I like to feel security, knowing that I can expand relationships and my circle of influence.
- I want to feel there is better harmony in my life so that I feel a sense of acceptance from others.
- I am calmed when my "street cred" and social ranking is boosted.

I'll admit I am prone to mood swings, so when my mood is moderated and I am calm, I am more open.

7. Adrenaline Seekers: Opportunists

I'm satisfied when I am calm. If I can see a "told you so" moment, I want to be rewarded with how I can participate. It's even more satisfying when I see how I can beat the system. It's especially important for me to feel that I'm in an exclusive group, an insider, and get in on the early action. I need to know up front that I'm going to learn something of value by consuming a marketer's message. When I feel I can learn something and benefit from a message without buying anything, I'm in. Of course what often happens is that I read an entire message, consume it, and find out I need just a little more information that can only be had by purchasing. I get it. If I want to have the full solution, it means I have to take the bait.

Here's what else I feel:

- An adrenaline rush is both stimulating and calming to me at the same time.
- When I decide to go for it, my mind goes into a trancelike state.
- I'm highly motivated when I live on the edge.
- As someone who lives for the adrenalin rush, disappointment can be intense, and I never want to experience that feeling.

My mind may never be totally calm, but if I feel satisfied that I'm going to get something out of it, I'll continue absorbing the marketing message.

8. Safe Players

I need to hear calming messages. My anxiety can be high, so I want to be quickly calmed. I warm up to organizations that very quickly show me how my money, health, relationships, and more will be safe with them. I want to be assured and reaffirmed that there is no risk.

Organizations should remember that with me they need to:

- Build my confidence to subdue my fears.
- Know that I'm content when I can find a product or service that helps to fulfill the promise of safety and security.
- Reassure that a proposition is no risk.

Guarantees are important to me because I value safety, above all else. I have to be moved away from the edge. Sometimes I like to see the guarantee early on in the sales message. It reassures me quickly. When I see that there is safety and security for myself and my loved ones, I am far more receptive to marketing messages.

9. Hiding My Compulsion

I seek calm, but my life always seems to be on the edge. That makes it hard for me to ever feel calm. Empathy works. Confidentiality around me works. The promise of a better day is hopeful. But I continue to feel there is a risk of being overpromised a transformation in my life. I've heard that before. It usually doesn't materialize. I want to have pressure eased in my life for just one day. There are a few ways that my mind can be calmed:

- I want to know that I am not alone. This is important to me. But I know that most people hide their secrets so well that it appears that no one else has a compulsion as I do.
- I need to be assured and comforted that an organization can be trusted.
- I want to be assured that there is safety and security by listening to an organization.

I will consider listening to a marketing message if it seems reasonable that I should take a chance with the organization. When I am calmed, I will slowly open up my trust. But I am fragile. Things must go slowly and easily. I may not respond quickly, but I will remember those who treat me with respect.

10. Fifty Plus

Despite my fears, as a baby boomer, I can still be calmed. The generation of baby boomers has always been hopeful and optimistic about the future. I just have to be promised that there are resources that will help me. I can be calmed by being reminded that compared to a generation ago, we're healthier and seeing advances only dreamed about by our parents. I see that I have options for a better life.

When I look at marketing messages:

- I want to be reminded that as a baby boomer we are still a reckoning force and relevant.
- I want to see continual breakthroughs, especially in health.

- I want to be assured there are answers for my problems as I enter new phases in my life.
- I want to be taken away, at least temporarily, from the worry of my financial future.

Deep down, I refuse to grow up. I don't see myself as slowing down or giving up. I want to feel like I am at least a decade younger than what I really am. And I want to feel that, as a baby boomer, I am helping to define a new era of people over 50.

11. Business 8 to 5

I am at my calmest when I'm able to just do my job without any interference. There is safety in continuing to use the same vendor, rather than finding a new vendor because it's a known entity. Changing vendors for anything in my company is risky for me. So I'm at my calmest when things are the status quo.

If a prospective vendor approaches me, I must be quickly reassured that a possible change could result in making me look good to my bosses. There needs to be proof that a change in relationship could benefit me. Still, I will proceed with caution even if I see an upside.

12. Did I Matter?

I want to feel that I can live on forever. That calms me. I understand there are varying degrees of how my legacy can be left. I realize that it is simple for some people. I deeply desire assurances that my inner circle of family and friends will remember me in a positive light. I know there are others who want to make a difference on a more global scale, often with complete strangers and anonymously. I want assurance that:

- My life is adding value to our world and culture.
- My life has been important.
- I will be remembered long after I am gone.

I am a multifaceted individual. I'm a person who is righteous in my belief. I'm careful with my money and thoughtful about cultivating my brand. But I am afraid that my legacy will be lost, so I need to have reason to see that my personal identity will be viewed as important.

Now let's turn to positioning (or repositioning) your product, service, and organization.

CHAPTER 7

POSITION/REPOSITION

Persona

Stimulate

Calm

Position

Story

Interpret

Permission

A unique selling proposition (USP), or unique value proposition (UVP), succinctly positions or repositions how you want to portray your story, your product, and your organization. It creates a strong, new memory about you, which, if effectively communicated, turns it into a long-term memory in the hippocampus. New long-term memory is essential to solidify your point. And new long-term memory can be more easily made with a USP or UVP.

UNIQUE SELLING PROPOSITION AND BRAND EQUITY

To drive home the importance of a unique selling proposition, it's useful to understand brand equity. Brand equity, by definition, reflects the real value of a brand name for its products or services. Establishing brand equity is essential because brands are believed to be strong influencers of critical business outcomes. Here are seven benefits of brand equity:[24]

- Be perceived differently and produce different interpretations of product performance.
- Enjoy greater loyalty and be less vulnerable to competitive marketing actions.
- Command larger margins and have more inelastic responses to price increases and elastic responses to price decreases.
- Receive greater trade cooperation and support.

- Increase marketing communication effectiveness.
- Yield licensing opportunities.
- Support brand extensions.

This idea of uniquely positioning a product originated in 1960, by Rosser Reeves. Reeves wrote a popular book called *Reality in Advertising*,[25] in which he defined the concept of unique selling proposition as: "Each advertisement must make a proposition to the consumer – not just words or product puffery. Every ad should tell the audience why they should buy and what specific benefit they will derive."

YOUR BRAND STATEMENT

What do your customers think of when they see your organization's name and logo? Your public image is important and should be up-to-date and fresh, especially during times of swift changes in technology, culture, and expectations from new generations. Every organization should go through a periodic review of its public perception and how it wants to be viewed by customers, donors, and prospects.

If you're like many organizations, you might not have a branding statement. This isn't to be confused with a mission statement (which can often be filled with empty language that rings hollow to customers and staff).

While sitting in the Board of Directors meeting for Vocal Majority (the chorus I have written about earlier), the topic came up of the desire to create a new logo. It was last updated in the 1990s, and even then, it still had 1970s visual remnants. It was agreed a new logo should be created, but it was also agreed that before going too far, a branding statement should be crafted to guide along the process more efficiently and result in a better outcome.

A branding statement is a marketing tool. It reflects your organization's reputation: what you are known for, or would like to be known for. It articulates how you stand apart from competitors. Often, individuals write a personal branding statement to define and enhance their own careers. If that's of interest to you, adapt the following steps, and you can be on your way to creating your personal branding statement.

In this section, I share ways to freshen your organization's brand and image. Here are ten steps:

1. **Audience Research.** Are you confident you accurately know the demographics, psychographics, and purchase behavior of your audience? If you've recently profiled or modeled your customers, then you probably have a good grasp of who they are. If it's been a year or longer, a profile is affordable and will yield a tremendous wealth of information about your customers. Demographics (age, income, education, etc.) are a good foundation. Knowing psychographics (personality, values, opinions, attitudes, interests, and lifestyles) takes you to another level. Knowing categories of purchase behavior enables you to drill down even further.

2. **Competitive Analysis.** You can't completely construct your own brand identity without understanding how your competitors position themselves. A competitive analysis can be conducted along two lines of inquiry: offline, such as analyzing direct mail and other print materials, along with what you can learn online. If you have print samples, you can discern much about a competitor's marketing message. But you may not be able to pin down demographics, psychographics, and purchase behavior by looking only at a direct mail package or print ad. There are a number of tools you can use online to deliver insights about your competition. Here are a few:

   a. Compete.com offers detailed traffic data so you can compare your site to other sites. You can also get keyword data, demographics, and more.

   b. Alexa.com provides SEO audits, engagement, reputation metrics, demographics, and more.

   c. Quantcast.com enables you to compare the demographics of who comes to your site versus your competitors. You'll be shown an index of how a website performs compared to the internet average. You'll get statistics on attributes such as age, presence of children, income, education, and ethnicity.

3. **Interpretation and Insight.** Now that you've conducted research, you're positioned to interpret the data to create your own insights. This is where creativity needs to kick in and where you need to consider the type of individual who will embrace and advocate for your organization. You may want to involve a few people from your team in brainstorming, or perhaps you'll want to bring in someone from outside your organization who can objectively look at your data. What's key is that you peer below the surface of the numbers and reports. Transform facts into insights through interpretation. Use comparison charts and create personas. Then create statements describing who your best customers are.

4. **One Word Description.** Now the challenging work begins. Distill your interpretation and insight into just one word that personifies your organization. Then think deeply about that word. Does it capture the essence of who you are (or want to become) and what your customer desires? For example, a technology company might use a word like "innovative," "cutting-edge," or "intuitive." Car manufacturers might use a one word description like "sleek," "utilitarian," or "safe" to describe their brand and what they want their customers to feel when they hear a brand's name. You might think that by only allowing one word, you are short-changing everything about your organization's image. It won't. Finding the one word that describes your organization's image will force you to focus.

5. **Reality Check.** So now you've identified a word to describe your organization's brand and image that resonates with both your team and your customers. It's time for a reality check. Can your organization or product actually support that word? If it's aspirational—that is, a word that you'd like your image to reflect in the future—is it achievable? And if it's aspirational, what plans are in place to take it to reality?

6. **Brand Promise and Benefits.** What do you promise that your customers will get from your brand? Is the promise of your brand and the actual benefit aligned? One way to do this is to list your promises and benefits side-by-side on a document or whiteboard. Place yourself in the shoes of your customer. See your brand features through their eyes. Then

ask yourself if you were the customer what you would get out of your promise. Keep drilling down and asking "why?"

7. **Emotional Promise and Benefits.** How does your customer feel when they see your brand? Ask yourself: "how does our brand make our customer feel?" Continue to ask the question, "why?" multiple times to get to a deeper emotional place. As a place to start a list of possible emotions, here are a few that your brand may mean to someone:
   a. Trustable
   b. Hopeful
   c. Happiness
   d. Sadness
   e. Fear
   f. Anger
   g. Hatred

8. **Credibility.** Your organization's brand must be credible. The customer only cares up to a certain point about what you do, so you must be believable and the real deal. What do customers say to you in testimonials? Your customers can be an excellent resource for identifying your positioning through their testimonials.

9. **Find Uniqueness.** You differentiate yourself from your competition by quality, price, service, reputation, story, or something else notably different. If you aren't positioned notably different on at least one of these, you will have a difficult time marketing your organization. You don't need a logical or rational difference. You need emotional differences. Your unique selling proposition paves the way to connect with your customers more deeply on an emotional level. Through positioning of your brand, or repositioning, you set yourself apart from your competitors. Importantly, you create an image that can be remembered more easily by your customers. It's a point of differentiation that helps you stand apart.

10. **Branding Statement Template.** By now you have pulled together a lot of information, and you are ready to create a branding statement. Here's a template to get you started:

The (Name of Organization or Individual) customer experiences (emotion). (Organization description in one sentence). (Short description of the audience). They are (more description of audience) and (description of how product is purchased and consumed). The one word that our customers will cite most often about (Name of Organization or Individual) is (sample of the top three words). We (delivery of your promise and benefit) so they feel good about (themselves or other elements). Our customers believe in (name of organization) because (emotional promise or other reasons), and they differentiate us from (competitors or organizations in your category) because (testimonials or other emotional take-away).

For Vocal Majority, this is how the branding statement came out:

The Vocal Majority musical experience is a refuge from the worries of the outside world. Vocal Majority is a non-profit men's chorus whose performers are volunteers. Our patrons are people who have a deep love of family and harmony—both in the musical sense, and in the cultural sense. Our audience is loyal and return again and again to listen to uplifting musical arrangements. They buy tickets to experience Vocal Majority at live performances, and purchase recordings to "take us home" with them. The words that our fans often use to describe Vocal Majority are harmony, excellence, and family. Our mission is to encourage and transform lives through vocal music. When people listen to Vocal Majority, they are inspired to feel good about themselves, their families, their beliefs and our country. We deeply touch the heart and soul. When Vocal Majority performs, the audience is transported to an oasis of positivity where they feel safe, comforted, and renewed.

With these steps, you're ready to create your own branding statement. When it's completed, distribute it to your staff, agency, or creative partners, and by all means, make sure you consistently deliver what your branding statement says about you.

POSITIONING BASED ON PERSONALITY TYPES

How you appeal to various personality types can be highly influenced by how you differentiate yourself from competitors. Consider the lens that each of these groups—intuitives, thinkers, feelers and sensors—will view your organization or brand:

- **Intuitives**. Desire new products or new experiences.
- **Thinkers.** Logical, sometimes put emotions aside, so they desire a reality check.
- **Feelers.** They look within themselves and can be influenced by testimonials.
- **Sensors.** Acutely aware of the world around them and assemble evidence.

Blend these traits within your organization's persona to strengthen your positioning or unique selling proposition. Consider, too, that people are usually a combination of each of these categories, and will migrate to different traits based on the organization or brand.

PROVEN WAYS TO CREATE A BLOCKBUSTER USP

A strong Unique Selling Proposition (USP) can produce more sales because it works to engrain new long-term memory. One way to differentiate yourself from your competitors is through repositioning your copy and design. If you haven't examined your USP lately, there's a good chance you're not leveraging your unique strengths as strategically as you could. Here are five proven ideas to help you refine your USP and create a blockbuster campaign.

Over the years, I've come to appreciate what the repositioning of a USP can do to skyrocket response. For a food gift company, we repositioned the product from the broad category of fruitcake to a Native Texas Pecan Cake. Sales increased 60 percent over the control in prospecting direct mail with a repositioned USP. For an insurance company, repositioning a modified benefit life insurance product, using an analysis of data, increased response 35 percent. For another campaign for a term life insurance product, response increased 60 percent.

First, it may be helpful to clarify what a Unique Selling Proposition is not:

- **Customer Service.** Great customer service doesn't qualify because your customer expects you'll provide great customer service and support in the first place.
- **Quality.** Like customer service, it doesn't qualify. It's expected.
- **Price.** You can never win if you think your USP is price and price cutting (or assume that a high price will signify better quality).

A strong USP boosts the brain's ability to absorb a new memory because you'll be seen as distinct from competitors.

Identifying your USP, which I'll also refer to as positioning, or repositioning an existing product or service, is a process. Most organizations should periodically reposition their product or service (or in the case of a non-profit, reposition why someone may be moved to contribute to your cause). Non-profits compete for dollars differently than, say, a marketer of shoes. If a marketer is selling shoes, that marketer is competing with other shoe retailers, not necessarily other apparel retailers. A non-profit fundraiser is likely competing for donations with every other fundraiser of interest to the prospective donor, along with other items or services wanted or needed. Having a strong USP can be the tie-breaker for a prospective donor. The challenge for fundraisers and every other marketer: identifying the USP for competitors comparing the results with your organization.

I have used the following five approaches to better understand buyers or donors and create a repositioned USP to deliver blockbuster results:

1. **Interview Customers and Prospects.** Talk directly with customers about why they have purchased or supported your organization. For contrast, talk directly with prospects about why they didn't act. You can interview by phone, but a better approach, in my experience, is in a focus group setting. Focus groups require a financial investment, so make sure you have two things in order: first, a completely considered and planned discussion guide of questions; and second, an interviewer who can

probe deeply with questions. Key word: "deeply." Superficial questions aren't likely to get what you want. Ask why a question was answered in a specific way, and then ask "why?" again and again. Your moderator must be able to continually peel back the onion, so to speak, to get to a deeper "why." Knowing the deeper "why" can be transformational for all concerned.

2. **Review Customer Data.** Profile your customer list. A profile can be obtained from many data bureaus to review more than basic demographics, to more deeply understand your customer's interests and behaviors. You need to understand what your customer does in their spare time, what they read and, to the degree possible, what they think. Getting a profile report is usually affordable, but the real cost may be in retaining someone from outside your organization to interpret the data on your behalf, draw inferences and conclusions, and transform raw numbers into charts and graphics to imagine the possibilities. If you have someone on your staff who can lead that charge, another option is to have discussions with your team as you review the data and commit to describing the persona of your best customer. Make this an ongoing process. You're not going to completely imagine and profile your customer in a one-hour meeting.

3. **Analyze Only Your Best Customers.** As a subset of the prior point, consider analyzing only your very top customers. You've heard of the Pareto Principle that suggests 80% of your business comes from 20% of your customers. Over the years, I've conducted many customer analyses, and have yet to find exactly an "80/20" balance. However, at the "flattest," I have found a 60/40 weighting, that is, 60% of a company's revenue coming from 40% of its customers (for a business-to-consumer marketer). At the other extreme, for a business-to-business corporation, the weighting was 90/10, where 90% of business came from just 10% of customers. Knowing this balance can be essential, too, to creating your position. If you were the organization who derived 90% of your business from just 10% of customers, chances are you'd listen very closely to only those 10% of customers as you

evaluate your position. In this instance, if you were to reposition your organization, the risk of a misfire is relatively large. Conversely, in the 60/40 weighted organization, repositioning may be less risky, since sales are spread across a greater number of customers, with a wider variety of expectations.

4. **Review Prospect Modeled Data.** If you are using modeled mailing lists, make sure you look at the subset of data you're mailing for the common characteristics of your best prospect. Like the profile of customers (mentioned in the previous point), you need to transform the data into charts and graphs to reveal trends and insights. Then, have a discussion and arrive at your interpretation of the results.

5. **Conduct a Competitive Analysis.** Examine a competitor's product or service and compare it to your product and offer. Be harsh on yourself. While conducting focus groups, you might allocate some of your discussion to your competitors and find out who buys from whom. As you look at your competitor's products, make sure you analyze their positioning in the market. Much can be learned from analysis of a competitor's online presence. Why online? Because what a competitor is doing online is easily accessible. If you have printed materials, use those, too.

Follow these steps to smartly reposition your USP, and you're on the way repositioning your own product or service that could deliver a new blockbuster campaign.

USING GAMIFICATION TO ESTABLISH POSITIONING

Marketers have known for years that involvement devices draw the reader in and often result in higher engagement and response. Our culture is obsessed with games and play. Look at casino gambling, or sporting events such as the Super Bowl. Marketers can seize the "gamification" phenomenon to position a product, and to another degree, enable customers to self-identify who they are.

On one side of the coin, games are used to reduce stress by people who play on mobile devices. An eMarketer[26] report said that 50 percent of mobile gamers spend up to 30 minutes daily playing games to reduce stress.

On the other side of the coin, offices use gamification to increase productivity, which reportedly increases stress. In office settings, gaming processes—gamification—engages users to solve problems that improve user engagement, ROI, data quality, timeliness and learning. An article in the Wall Street Journal titled "The 'Gamification' of the Office Approaches"[27] noted how productivity inside offices can be tracked and measured in points, fostering competitiveness and excellence.

Gaming is all around us. Millions scratch off lottery tickets or pick random numbers, and casinos are often packed.

Every year, the biggest football game of the year—the Super Bowl—is played with millions watching, and a lot of money wagered, as it becomes a national obsession for several days.

Let's face it: We're a culture who loves to play games and keep score.

For marketers, you can use our cultural obsession with games for a marketing advantage to increase engagement and sales.

Whether you use offline direct mail with tokens or other involvement devices, or online channels, legally vetted gaming techniques can be a good way to perk up your results.

Here are five ideas for using gamification to position your product differently from your competitors:

1. In direct mail, if you mail your prospects or customers frequently, add a game that builds over time for purpose, more interaction and anticipation of your mailing.

2. For any channel you're in, use games to create customer loyalty so your buyers return again and again.

3. In social media, check-ins and badges using mobile apps are like games, and they get your name in front of the friends of your fans.

4. Encourage people to play a game that requires completing surveys and gives information about themselves for use in nurture marketing

programs where email, direct mail or other channels are used to "drip" content over time.

5. Let your prospects and customers track their game scores, but as a marketer using sophisticated marketing automation software, you can turn the tables and score your customers to determine who is most likely to come back and buy again.

Finally, if you're stumped with generating ideas, get your staff together and play games to get the ideas swirling. Ideation meetings that include games often bring out unexpected creative ideas.

Bottom line, use the principles of gamification to create a unique positioning and re-energize your marketing approach. By becoming familiar with gamification techniques now, you might identify the next big repositioning of your product that results in being a sales game changer.

To summarize, you must position/reposition your product's benefits that your competition doesn't offer, such as a uniqueness of brand or a new claim. Your unique selling proposition must be so strong that it will compel customers to shift to your product. Use the tips and techniques from this chapter and you'll be on your way to breaking away from your competition, and get the attention of your customer's mind.

USP IDEAS FOR THE 12 PERSONAS

Returning to the 12 personas, here are ideas about how you can position, or reposition:

1. Trailblazers/Early Adopters

If you want my attention, products must be positioned as being new, innovative, and leading-edge. And you must make good on that positioning. I'll turn a product away if it looks like yesterday's news or breakthrough. There's a lot of competition out there, and if you want my loyalty, don't let a competitor beat you to the punch with a newer and sexier positioning statement. So you'd better be researching your competition and compare your product, because if you don't, I will.

I have a short attention span, so product positioning needs to be freshened often to stay ahead of the curve. I expect the companies I rely upon to have regular brainstorming and planning to review the existing product position, figure out what's out-of-date, and strategize about how the next bright, shiny object is going to be created.

2. My Brand/My Lifestyle/My Growth

I like to see that an organization has my best interest at heart. I'm concerned about styles and priorities changing with every season. It's vital to me that any company I do business with is current and with the times. I look for an organization as a resource to enhance my personal brand and my perceived trademark.

My friends and my relationships are important to me. I tend to band together with people who think like me. We are highly interactive and we can be snarky about those who appear to be yesterday's news. I want to stand apart from the crowd. I seek out products and services that will deliver uniqueness. I don't want to be a copycat. I don't want to see a company claiming something to be their own, but learning it was ripped it off from someplace else. When I find a company that is unique and serves my needs, I'll end up doing the selling for them!

3. Money Matters

A product positioned with value is essential for me. I want to see that I am smart when I buy from an organization. When I see that an investment will pay off over time, that can be a strong positioning to me. I must see fundamental intrinsic value that will appeal to my very core. My pragmatism is very deeply ingrained, so anything I see shouldn't be extravagant or particularly flashy. I like down-to-earth. For example, when I contribute to a specific type of cause, I want to see it demonstrated that most of my financial gift will flow to the people or the situation where money is intended to go.

I like to accumulate financially smart assets. Things are not very important to me. I like to research information. It's very helpful when a marketer positions themselves as the resource of the best information. A marketer sharing research for me is helpful. But that information must be credible. I will seek independent validation of anything that is claimed by a marketer's positioning. I'm adept at numbers so I will look for facts and costs in a matter-of-fact, pragmatic kind of way. That's how I will most likely accept a marketer's message.

4. On Financial Edge

I'm most comfortable working with people and an organization that understands my problem and won't take advantage of my situation. I want to feel that they have my best interests at heart. A company that approaches me in a trusting way, that offers a helping hand, and is not judgmental means a lot to me.

I want to be talked to in plain language, but don't talk down to me! My reading skills aren't the best, so I need to be able to understand any terms or conditions. Hearing a message sometimes is the best for me. I like to talk to people in person or at least hear a recorded message or watch a video.

I don't want to feel like I am being investigated if I need money or credit. I want my life to be private, and an organization who can reassure me of my privacy is important.

5. Right Thing to Do: Taking the High Road

It's important to me that I see a company's core values prominently displayed. I want to know that this organization is credible and trustable. I seek high standards. I don't expect any more from an organization than I would personally deliver or stand by if the roles were reversed. I will be loyal to a company who is positioned within the scope of my values. I want the internal satisfaction that the decisions I make are aligned with that of anyone I do business with. I have strong work ethics and character. I want a better tomorrow, so it's essential that a product is positioned for making the world a better place.

6. Love and Social Relationships

A marketer's positioning needs to support my deep internal need for building relationships. Make a promise and demonstrate that by engaging with a marketer's product or service that my life will be more fulfilled.

I'm sensitive to my credibility so a marketer must constantly illustrate in its positioning how it supports me. I warm up to positioning that:

- Enhances love and the experience with my partner.
- Strengthens relationships.
- Elevates my "street cred."

7. Adrenaline Seekers: Opportunists

I want to see a path toward winning, so I want to see opportunities positioned for me that are exclusive and offered on a limited time basis. I'm selfish, and I don't want to share in the joy of victory; I want to be able to boast about it. Turn me into a winner and deliver on it, and a company will have me as a customer for life.

But I'm not easily snookered into things. I need to see that there is a track record where others have been successful. I like to read testimonials and have other winners shown. When that happens, the message is more credible to me. I seek authority, especially if I'm investing my money. But I also admit to being a high roller wannabe when the bright lights sparkle.

I want to see action and possibility. When I do, I will give an organization the time of day. But if I don't get quick results or have a quick win, I'll move on. I want to know that an organization will help me feed my passion.

8. Safe Players

I need to see safety in a marketing message. It's essential. There simply can be no risk for me. Anything that can be done that boosts my self-confidence is an extra bonus. I feel more assured with guarantees and testimonials, but I must feel that the positioning of a company is sincere and authentic. When an organization points out how outcomes can be worse if I fail to take action, I will listen.

9. Hiding My Compulsion

A positioning of empathy works for me. Too often, marketers charge right into their message without taking into account my thoughts and feelings. A marketer must be gentle. A USP that assures me I am not alone with my compulsion will often engage me. I am drawn to safety, and in messaging I want to have the opportunity to see myself as a hero. I need a friend, and that can be communicated through a company's positioning.

10. Fifty Plus

I am engaged with marketer's product positions when my unique situation and phase of my life is acknowledged. My mind encompasses so many concerns spanning from health and wealth to lifestyle, along with being an empty nester and caring for a parent. I have multitudes of concerns.

I want to see positioning that recognizes and identifies my relative age, and then helps to offer me a place that defines my life in a new and better way. A few of those ideas include:

- Mentally transforming me to a place where I can feel younger, but don't dwell on reminding me of my youth from decades ago.
- An organization that can help me with the burdens of life today.

Make no mistake: I have fond memories of the 1960s and 70s. I get nostalgic sometimes. Those were turbulent times in American history; not unlike what we experience today. I've been there, and I've done that. But I still want to be taken to a place of happy memories. I like a bit of nostalgia because it's fun to be taken back to a time that I wish I could relive again.

11. Business 8 to 5

I need to know that a prospective vendor can fulfill my company's requirements. In situations where I am happy with the current vendor, I need to understand how a new vendor is unique. In situations where I am not satisfied with the current vendor, I need to understand how a new vendor will be different and better than the status quo. Either way, I must see how a company's product or service is decidedly different from what I'm currently doing now before I will give them the time of day.

12. Did I Matter?

I am open to the positioning statement of an organization that offers to show me how my money will be used well. I'm also open to making plans now for the future. Just remember, though: I'm not dead yet! So I am sensitive to those who suggest otherwise.

I continue to weigh many options in my life. I look at a multitude of organizations so that I know there is competition for my dollars. But I want to see that I will be honored for years to come. I want to see that the cause or the product I'm being offered promises to fill an emptiness for the rest of my life.

Now let's turn to storytelling.

CHAPTER 8

STORYTELLING

Persona

Stimulate

Calm

Position

Story

Interpret

Permission

Use storytelling to convert the new short-term memory created with positioning/repositioning, into long-term memory in the hippocampus. With an engaging story and a new angle, you can magnetically pull the individual into the storyline so they are a participant and see themselves having a role. This creates a new perspective and memory. Importantly, it creates new grooves in the brain for recall.

THE SCIENCE BEHIND WHY STORYTELLING WORKS

Earlier, I shared with you why I'm so curious about the brain and how it works. But I didn't share with you the story of how my life as a compulsive hair puller began, and the deep groove it has engrained in my mind.

It was after noon the day it first happened. I remember it like it was yesterday. A warm fall day in 1962 — probably in October, and probably about the time of my sixth birthday when I was in the 1st Grade. It was harvest season on the farm; that time of year when Dad would harvest the crops. When it was harvest season, there was urgency in the air because the crops were ready and the weather could turn any day, making it difficult to bring in the fall harvest—the paycheck that we had waited for so long to be able to collect.

We had a 1951 GMC pick-up truck called Jimmy. We also called it the Red Horse because it had been used many times in the pasture to help round up cattle.

During harvest, neighbors helped each other if they could. Our neighbor Bill, who was nearing retirement, was helping Dad that day. I don't know what he was doing, or why he was driving Jimmy, but I do remember that he invited me to ride along to the field to watch Dad combine milo, a crop grown to feed to livestock.

I climbed in the back of the truck. There were boards on the side and across the top so it was completely enclosed. The back of the truck had been cleaned out, so perhaps I rode there for the novelty of being in back and completely surrounded by the boards. I couldn't possibly get out. There must have been a fascination with riding in the back. Who knows? I was only about six, doing illogical things that small children do.

Bill drove into the milo field that had just been harvested. The field was rough, and there were ruts in the earth from rainfall during the spring and summer after the crops had been planted. Jimmy, the truck, didn't have shocks, or if it did, they were completely worn out.

The field was bumpy. But as we drove through it, one rut was apparently deeper than most and, as we hit it, I was thrown and hit my head on the boards above. It wasn't enough to knock me out, but it was enough to cause a welt to appear above my left ear.

It hurt. But a few days later, I discovered that gently touching it gave me a sense of peace. It felt good to stroke it. Soothing. Calming.

Touching the welt was so peaceful, and so serene, that for motivations and reasons I'll never know, I suddenly pulled a hair. Maybe I was experimenting just to see how it would feel. Maybe it was accidental. It doesn't matter. Pulling that hair felt good. It gave me a tingling rush.

Pulling that hair was soothing to the welt and it gave me a euphoric emotional lift. It felt so good that I pulled another hair. And another. And I continued pulling. I don't know how long I pulled, but time became meaningless as I pulled my hair.

In a short period of time I had pulled enough hair to leave a circular shaped bald spot about the size of a dime. The welt was exposed. The skin was smooth to the touch of my fingertips and I was fascinated with the sensation. I couldn't see the damage until I was back in the house and looked in a mirror. I was stunned to see what I had done. I knew that I had to hide it, so I combed my hair over the bald spot. Even though I was only six, I knew that pulling hair wasn't natural.

That day was the start of a lifetime of emotional turmoil, zigzagging from the highs of hair pulling euphoria to the depths of devastation for what I had done. It would be a day that I wish I could take back and had never experienced — a day that would forever alter the fabric of my soul.

THE EIGHT SECOND ATTENTION SPAN

I share this deeply personal story to hold your attention and set the stage for this chapter. You see, most people's attention spans are short. As shared in Chapter 5, it's only eight seconds.

So how do you heighten your odds of someone sticking with you beyond eight seconds? You tell a story.

And how do you increase the value of your product? By telling a story.

A *New York Times*[28] article captures and conveys the mechanics of how a great story can enhance the value of a product. In one instance, a writer bought an unremarkable Russian figure at a garage sale for three dollars.

He posted it for sale on eBay, but unlike most eBay sellers who include a short, factual paragraph or bullet points listing color, size, and other features, he made up an elaborate story to romance the product, engage the reader, and make it more interesting. He dreamed up a story about the figurine, naming it Saint Vralkomir, with a story about how the figurine comes to life on moonless winter nights. The writer clearly states in the eBay posting that the entire yarn was fabricated. Yet, the writer actually sold the item, on eBay, for $193.50.

What do stories do to the brain that causes such a reaction?

Consider how stories have the ability to change a person's life. Whether hearing a story casually from a friend, or from a presenter giving a keynote speech, or reading it in a book, biological changes are made in the mind. Those changes can linger for a few days. Or when deep-seated enough, such as an event triggering a compulsion like pulling hair, the story and memory can last for a lifetime.

In a study conducted by the Emory Institute in Atlanta[29] researchers asked 21 students to participate in a functional Magnetic Resonance Imaging scan (fMRIs) to examine if there would be increased connectivity in the area of the brain associated with language (the left temporal cortex), and if there would be lingering neural effects, from reading a story. During the first five days, scans were taken of the initial brain structure. Then over the next nine days, the students were asked to read the novel *Pompeii*.

Pompeii[30] is a 2003 thriller by Robert Harris based on the real-life eruption of Mount Vesuvius in ancient Italy. The lead author of the study, Gregory Berns, says, "the story follows a protagonist, who is outside the city of Pompeii and notices steam and strange things happening around the volcano. He tries to get back to Pompeii in time to save the woman he loves. Meanwhile, the volcano continues to bubble and nobody in the city recognizes the signs."

The book was chosen because of its page-turning plot. "It depicts true events in a fictional and dramatic way," Berns says. "It was important to us that the book had a strong narrative line."

When scans were taken over the remaining five days, they revealed increased brain activity. The research also suggested that thinking about an action triggers the very same areas that are active while actually performing the action.

Stories create physical changes to the brain. In the case of the Emory Institute study, Berns said, "the neural changes that we found associated with physical sensation and movement systems suggest that reading a novel can transport you into the body of the protagonist."

Reality: a mass of cold hard data doesn't engage the brain. Story does. Story is like glue that holds together your message. While numbers and facts can activate the brain, engagement occurs through powerful words and stories. And engagement helps the brain store information.

THREE STAGES OF HOW THE BRAIN STORES INFORMATION

Perhaps the best metaphor to describing how the brain stores information is to describe how a computer works. When you add a picture to your computer, it must be uploaded, or encoded, into the system. Then it's stored in memory (the hard drive, or the cloud). When you want to look at the picture later, you send a command to retrieve it from memory.

Encode. Store. Retrieve. It's important to understand and remember these three stages of how the brain stores a memory, because it will reinforce the reason behind why story is so important. Let's now dive into each in more detail.

Stage 1: Memory Encoding

The first stage to create a memory is encoding. It happens in the hippocampus, which you learned earlier is associated with memory. It influences four sensations:

1. Visual
2. Auditory
3. Smell
4. Touch

When you activate all four of these senses—each with its own unique contribution—you more deeply encode the memory because of the integration of these perceptions. Experts believe that your brain analyzes these senses in both the hippocampus and frontal cortex to sort out what is worth remembering.

So as a marketer working through the mind's pathways to create new memory grooves, the first thing you need to accept is that perceptions are the foundation of a person's memory. You've probably heard the axiom "Perception is reality." Well, it's true. Whatever the perception of the individual may be, it is the reality they are feeling. If the facts don't justify the position, it will be an uphill climb to change it.

Here's why: as a memory begins with a perception, nerve cells connect with other cells at a point called a synapse. Electrical pulses in the synapse carry messages that move across gaps between cells.

As pulses move, a neurotransmitter, or a chemical messenger, attaches to nearby cells. Dendrites—feathery tips of brain cells—are segments of the neuron that receive stimulation in order for the cell to become active. The dendrites reach out to these neurotransmitters. Then the cells work together, network, and organize themselves into groups. As signals are sent between brain cells, they are amplified. The more signals, the more strength. So with new experiences, the brain slightly rewires and organizes and reorganizes itself in response to the experience or message, forming new memories.

Repetition of the information or use of that information reinforces the memory. Think about when you last memorized something—perhaps a song. If you were singing it, you know that continued practice reinforces the memory to make its recall and replication flawless. How else would you explain how professional performers remember the lyrics and notes of a song in front of thousands of fans? If you know the lyrics of a song, perhaps you sing to yourself in the shower. Hear the song over and over, and it deepens grooves and engrains memory. But what if you stop singing that song? Over time you gradually realize that you don't know it as well as you once did. The brain has started the slow process of forgetting what you once had memorized.

If you want to properly encode memory (whether it's your personal memory, or you're attempting to influence a memory of a prospective customer), you, or the person you're reaching, must be engaged. You constantly filter information. In fact, only a small percentage of your daily stimuli are actually recognized. Think of the overload you (and your prospects) feel, if at the end of the day, you remembered everything you experienced. People remember what is significant to them, and importantly, that significance is influenced by how they or your prospect paid attention to the information.

Now that the memory has been encoded, it needs to be stored.

Stage 2: Memory Storage
This is the second stage of the process.

You're in the midst of creating a new memory. Maybe your message was so impactful that the memory is already deeply engrained. More likely, you need to reinforce the memory with a more in-depth story.

Now the memory you're creating with your marketing message must be stored for later retrieval.

There are three ways memories can be stored:

1. **Sensory Information Storage (SIS).** Senses for memory use begins with sight, touch, hearing, sight, or smell. The SIS, as a split-second holding cell for all sensory information, explains why a video shot at multiple frames per second seems to be continually moving instead of a series of distinct pictures. With an avalanche of information bombarding us, the SIS allows the brain to process a sensory event for a little longer than the extent of the duration itself. This means most of what people sense is forgotten immediately, unless you do something with the memory.

2. **Short-Term Memory.** It's temporary. For example, you go to the gym where you pick a random locker to store your belongings. An hour or so later when you return to the locker room, you're able to go right to the locker, but once you leave the facility, you quickly forget the locker number. Or you check into a hotel and are assigned a room number. You remember the room number until you check out. The average short-term memory can hold a handful of units; in fact, experts believe the average people hold is just seven units. Is it no coincidence that phone numbers (excluding the area code) are exactly seven digits? For marketers who use broadcast media, once you start the memory of a toll-free area code (800 is still the gold standard for a toll-free number for this short-term memory reason), you have a better shot that the short-term memory persists long enough for a prospective customer to call. When the telephone number is repeated over and over, it keeps resetting the short-term memory clock of the listener. Another tip with phone numbers: chunk the numbers—that is, separate them into groups—using hyphens for separation. For example, 800-555-1234.

3. **Long-Term Memory.** When you deem something important, or something happens that is highly impactful (whether you want to remember it or not), that information is transferred from short-term memory into long-term memory, and, of course, retained. Normally,

an unlimited amount of long-term memory can be stored, often indefinitely. Because people can more easily store memory related to subjects they are already familiar with, someone with even an average memory can remember a great deal about certain subjects.

Taken another step, long-term memory can be divided even further.

- **Declarative Memory.** These are conscious memories you have to make an effort to remember.
  - ○ **Semantic Memory.** General knowledge you store. For example, how you recall the names of the capitals of each of the 50 U.S. states.
  - ○ **Episodic Memory.** Recall of specific events, such as remembering what you did for a milestone birthday.

Both Semantic and Episodic memories serve as information processing systems that selectively receive information, retain some aspects of information, and transfer specific information to other systems, including the systems that turn the information into behavior and conscious awareness. These systems also differ in how they store and retrieve information.

- **Non-Declarative Memory.** These are unintentional memories you store.
  - ○ **Procedural Memories.** These are memories of how to perform certain motor skills, such as riding a bicycle.
  - ○ **Conditioned Memories.** When stimuli such as lights, sounds, and smells can predict various important events such as knowing that when lightning strikes, the sound of thunder will soon follow. Or, knowing that when you turn on the stove, the burner will soon get hot.

While on this topic, here's one more very unusual long-term memory type that deserves mention. It is eidetic memory, or more casually referred to as a photographic memory. As an example, a person with eidetic memory can see a list of 70 digits for less than a minute, then recount the list forwards and backwards and remember it for years.

Once these various types of memories are stored, they can be retrieved for later reference.

Stage 3: Memory Retrieval

This is the final stage in memory encoding.

When you've done a great job of communicating your message and it is stored so deeply that your customers will remember you and your product, you reach a level that few marketers achieve. To get there, you need to register the memory deeply.

As an example, consider your memory of where you left your house keys. How many times have you set them down, only to realize that just minutes later you need them and you can't find them? In this scenario, any of these things could have happened:

- You may not register clearly where you put them down to begin with.
- You may not retain what you registered.
- You may not be able to retrieve the memory accurately.

However, with engagement of your memory system, you can set your keys down and later remember exactly where you put them.

Therefore, if you want to remember where you set down your keys, you have to engage the three stages of the memory encoding process. Forgetting something means encoding the memory wasn't done effectively, possibly because of distraction or interruption when the encoding should have taken place. To your detriment, the location of your keys may never have made it initially into your memory.

Taken to another level for marketing, if someone is reading or absorbing your message and they are distracted, chances are, the memory won't be effectively saved. There's nothing you can do about distraction of prospective customers, but you greatly enhance memory when your story is engaging, your customer returns, re-engages, and remembers your message.

With this greater understanding of the three-stage process of memory encoding—encode, store, and retrieve—you're better prepared to create a strong marketing strategy.

ANCIENT STORYTELLING TECHNIQUES

Storytelling has been a part of human culture for a very long time. In fact, you can look back centuries to see how to use story to mesmerize and hold attention.

Ancient Greek and Shakespearean storytelling drama actually have much to do with marketing and selling—perhaps more than you realize. Let's dissect a proven five-step process that has been used for centuries to hold the reader until the end of a story. You can use this timeless framework for writing compelling storytelling copy that engages and sells. But first, a bit of background.

Marketers clamor to have their message go viral. You want your customers to become advocates and evangelists. You want them to "like," comment, and share your message. A mention on the evening news can skyrocket the number of views on an online video into the tens of millions, often for a "feel good" moment.

How do you reach the masses? Most likely through effective storytelling, since it's less likely your hard-hitting sales message is going to be shared or discussed.

Personally, I think storytelling can be used by marketers today as part of the "'for good' movement" that has permeated culture, largely fueled by social media. Your challenge is how to engage through story, and effectively monetize these efforts better than your competitors.

For example, I completed an analysis for Vocal Majority, an organization that balances "'for good movement" messaging with selling. In this case, the "for good movement" messages drive interest and traffic from videos of performance and behind-the-scenes stories. I have seen the interest build and go viral in the likes, comments, and shares of certain types of social media messaging. More importantly, it translates into more web traffic. More web traffic results in more event and product sales. The numbers don't lie.

A few illustrations:

- An informal video, recorded on an iPad and uploaded to YouTube, of Vocal Majority performing for a boy wounded in a school shooting, and posted on Facebook and Twitter, is watched thousands of times in just a few days. Nothing was sold here—just the "feel good" story. Watch it at CustomerMindCode.com/Resources.
- A behind-the-scenes interview is watched by thousands so fans get something they don't hear elsewhere. The video closes with a reminder of an upcoming performance. Again, nothing sold here—just insider information shared. Watch it at CustomerMindCode.com/Resources.
- A static post overtly selling an upcoming performance doesn't get much traction in likes, comments, and shares. That doesn't mean it was a failure. It simply says that people don't want to be sold. They want to choose to buy. And in this case, people choose to buy more enthusiastically when a series of stories lead up to the event.

People want to be part of a movement, and when they can experience that at an event, they are ready and willing to buy. When a product is available for sale at the event, demand exists because the customer is ready to buy before you ask them to buy.

With that distinction in selling style, it's vital that you don't forget to strategically weave a monetization component into a "for good" message. That doesn't mean that you add an intrusive sales pitch in the message. It means that you naturally lead your customers and prospects through a planned sequence, timed in a way that takes the individual to the ultimate goal: purchase.

Now, back to the five-step process to hold the reader until the end of the story. Inspiration for my thoughts leading up to this list came from an article in the *Harvard Business Review* titled "The Irresistible Power of Storytelling as a Strategic Business Tool."[31] It explains this process in Freytag's Pyramid[32] which has been a successful storytelling framework, going back centuries.

Using your imagination, you can see how it applies to marketing copywriting and story:

1. **Exposition.** The exposition is the portion of a story that introduces important background information to the audience; for example, information about the setting, events occurring before the main plot, characters' back stories, etc. Convey exposition through dialogues, flashbacks, character's thoughts, background details, or the narrator telling a back-story.

2. **Rising Action.** In the rising action, a series of related incidents build toward the point of greatest interest. The rising action of a story is the series of events that begin immediately after the exposition of the story and builds up to the climax. These events are generally the most important parts of the story since the entire plot depends on them to set up the climax, and ultimately, the satisfactory resolution of the story itself.

3. **Climax.** The climax is the turning point, which changes the protagonist's fate. If the story is a comedy, things will have gone badly for the protagonist up to this point; now, the plot will begin to unfold in his or her favor, often requiring the protagonist to draw on hidden inner strengths. If the story is a tragedy, the opposite state of affairs will ensue, with things going from good to bad for the protagonist, often revealing the protagonist's hidden weaknesses.

4. **Falling Action.** During the falling action, the conflict between the protagonist and the antagonist unravels, with the protagonist winning or losing against the antagonist. The falling action may contain a moment of final suspense, in which the final outcome of the conflict is in doubt.

5. **Denouement.** The denouement comprises events from the end of the falling action to the actual ending scene of the drama or narrative. Conflicts are resolved, creating normality for the characters and a sense of catharsis, or release of tension and anxiety, for the reader.

As you read these five-steps, you can probably visualize how they flowed in a favorite movie or book. The next time you read a fiction novel or watch a movie, chances are good you'll see this storytelling process used.

There is another reason why storytelling is so powerful: it's the emotion you can evoke. This insightful quote (shared earlier in this book) from author Maya Angelou succinctly sums up why storytelling in copywriting is so important:

> *"I've learned that people will forget what you said, people will forget what you did, but people will never forget how you made them feel."*

Effective copy used in storytelling, and the "for good movement," leads to feeling good. And leading people to feel good is how you as a marketer move them to respond.

STORYTELLING-IN-CONTENT MARKETING LESSONS LEARNED

People hold their attention spans longer when they find something enjoyable or intrinsically motivating. This means that if your marketing message is relevant, interesting, entertaining, and fun, your prospect's attention will be sustained.

Storytelling lifts content marketing into more powerful messaging. I have learned ten lessons as a result of a content marketing campaign that I oversaw for Vocal Majority. It was designed to energize volunteers and followers, build a larger base of supporters, and strengthen a brand with the long-term goal of monetization through product and event sales.

First, some background.

During this campaign, I had seen, first-hand, the power of story with diverse styles of online video content marketing, including interviews and behind-the-scenes stories that build up to a major event, along with the high viewership of the final long-form video.

Since Vocal Majority is a music-based organization, and because video is frequently used as the primary messaging vehicle, I've come to realize the power of not only music, but overlaying storytelling.

After a six-month pre-contest campaign had concluded, I came to realize that I learned ten lessons from this campaign about storytelling and content marketing.

1. **Stimulate Interest/Earn Trust.** Your audience probably isn't interested in what you have to sell until you have stimulated their interest and earned their trust in your contribution to making their lives better.

2. **Give Them Unusual Access.** They want to be let in on what's behind the scenes. Video can deliver this experience better than any other channel.

3. **Build Tension/Release With Joy.** Like any good story, add an element of tension, but let the audience experience joy. Again, as author Maya Angelou said, people will remember you for how you made them feel.

4. **Give Context in Your Story.** As an insider and storyteller, it is your responsibility to set the stage. You should refrain from using acronyms and jargon, so that the viewer can appreciate the importance of the story's upcoming element.

5. **Leverage the Fear of Missing Out (FOMO).** Craft your story to make it build from one part to the next, so your audience, while fearing they'll miss something, is looking for your message.

6. **Let Characters Be the Stars.** If you have multiple people in the story, creatively develop a delivery vehicle so everyone can participate. (One crazy idea worked out well, about how to include over 140 people, including myself, in a video. Watch it at CustomerMindCode.com/Resources).

7. **Put Your Audience Inside the Story.** Don't be detached. Invite them to come along with you.

8. **Encourage Comments and Reviews.** Your audience will tell you what they think, so invite participation.

9. **The Story Dictates Length.** Many claim videos must be short. That's not necessarily true. They must be tightly edited and move the story along. The final video in this series lasted 36 minutes. Watch "On That Day" at CustomerMindCode.com/Resources. YouTube audience retention was higher than average, all the way to the end. Use YouTube analytics to reveal where fall-offs occur and to improve your overall storytelling.

10. **Strategically Monetize.** Think long-term about monetizing content marketing. In this series of videos and story leading up to a climax, coming into the all-important fourth quarter of the year, this audience

was pumped. This made the job of selling performance tickets, recordings, and fundraising easier.

Beyond building the brand (and winning the international contest), tangible results of this six-month campaign included combined video views in the tens of thousands (and still growing), website views spiking by four times over average, consistently strong email open and click rates, Facebook Fan page follower increase of 25 percent, and a Twitter follower increase of 27 percent.

Bottom line: You must continue to offer multiple reasons for people to return to your website. You do that by developing a compelling story and content.

Finally, a word about music and the brain, and why this storytelling campaign was so successful: Brain imaging studies are telling us more about the importance of singing or playing a musical instrument than we've known before. For instance, if you're a manager or executive, chances are that as a child you sang or played a musical instrument. Emotions encouraged by music activate frontal brain regions and can have a significant impact on your marketing messaging.

Music has the power to create a pleasurable experience that sends "chills." As chills increase, many changes in cerebral blood flow are seen in brain regions such as the amygdala. These same brain areas appear to link to reward, motivation, emotion and arousal, and are also activated in other pleasurable situations, including the pleasure a person can feel from buying.

Storytelling works. The inclusion of relevant music in storytelling can stimulate and take people to desirable emotional places. If you want reaction, make sure the music sends "chills."

USING STORY FOR THE 12 PERSONAS

Here are storytelling ideas for each of the 12 personas:

1. Trailblazers/Early Adopters

I think I'm pretty cool, especially with technology. But you know, I like to hear a good story, too. As long as there is a point, you can engage me and I'll even stick with you. But don't waste my time.

Tell me a story about how I can be envied by my friends. Or tell me how I can anticipate being the first to get a product with the anticipation and joy of having it.

But I want the story to feel like I'm the star. I want to walk right into the story line. I'll probably empathize with the hero of the story, and I'm going to remember a good story for a while (and might just tell it over and over to my friends).

2. My Brand/My Lifestyle/My Growth

I have a great imagination. I like to hear stories from companies I do business with. They can set themselves apart by being unique. That is deeply desirable to me.

Because I am brand and style conscious, the story can include a role model. I like to hear about people who have come from struggle and who have succeeded with changes in their lives. I like to know an organization has had that same "come from behind" experience. This helps enable me to know that my own doubts can be overcome. As someone interested in personal growth, sometimes I doubt my own ability to achieve goals. I want to see that people just like me can achieve the same goals that I have. I like to know that someone has turned around their life because of certain decisions and actions that they have taken. This makes the story credible.

I like to hear stories about how someone's life was changed because their look caught the eye of a lover, employer, or someone who could make them famous. I'm drawn to photographs, illustrations, and elegant design.

3. Money Matters

A sensible story resonates for me. The tone of the story needs to feature someone like me who is unassuming, who doesn't flaunt possessions, and quietly lives their lives knowing that they make smart choices. I'm fine with hearing about someone who is wealthy as long as they are not flashy. Their story can be a template for my story. I like to hear things like that.

I want to see that nothing is wasted. I want the story to substantiate claims credibly. The story is even enhanced if I can see how someone was not taken advantage of.

I can be a numbers geek, so I like data woven into a story. Include charts, graphs, and numbers, and you can keep me engaged for a long time. When I'm thinking like an investor, for example, I'm drawn to a story that illustrates how insider information or hidden information was used to make significant money. Metaphors help, too. This helps me connect the dots between myself and what a company is offering.

Most important in the story is that I must see a value message. The cost is less important to me than the value it returns. Sure, I'm interested in a deal. But that doesn't necessarily mean cheap.

4. On Financial Edge

There are so many people just like me. I like to hear how an organization has helped someone in a situation like mine. The story should tell me how easy it is to do business with a company who understands that I need non-traditional approaches. It's important to me that an organization empathizes with my situation. When I see a testimonial from someone else, it helps to reassure me and I'm more apt to give this organization a chance. Stories are important to me. Sometimes I feel so alone, and with so few lifelines, that hearing how others were helped will make me feel better.

5. Right Thing to Do: Taking the High Road

I enjoy reading stories about people who have a deep desire to do the right thing. These people are my heroes. There are people who would save a life. I want to be just like those people because in my heart I believe that every good deed is rewarded.

When I can identify with a hero, no matter what the product, I am engaged in the message. I need to know this story exists so that there are no regrets in making a purchase. I want to know that someone felt better about himself or herself and could sleep better at night. I want to know that my pride and my moral compass are strong. I want to see how mediocrity can be overcome. I believe that ethics and character will always prevail. When the story is strong, the cost of the product doesn't matter to me.

I'm especially drawn to stories where someone has created a movement, or a persuasive way to advance a position. Big ideas enthrall me. When I see myself in the story and see my role as part of something larger, I will buy quickly and participate almost without question.

6. Love and Social Relationships

My emotion is aroused when I hear a story about romance with a dose of eroticism. This brings me more deeply into the message because it affirms my feeling about love. Sometimes I go into a trance, and I deeply desire to be part of a story like that. My life sometimes has emptiness and I want to know that there are other people who share my feelings. I want to know that other people experience moments like these in their lives. But I want to see goodness for other people so that I can see the light of day shining on myself.

A story can help to alleviate my insecurities. I like to share stories on social media. I like to be the first to get the news out fast so I look like I am a trend setter, and not a follower. This elevates my mood. I consider it a selfie moment.

7. Adrenaline Seekers: Opportunists

I want to hear a private story; one that I feel is just for me, and no one else. A story heightens my senses. A story tells me how someone made it big, with the inside secrets of getting there.

I crave having a plan that is unconventional. I believe I can go into it alone and not follow mainstream thought. So a marketer's story needs to bring to life either someone or something that shows me how it's done without the establishment. I view money as a scorecard, so a marketer's story is of most interest when it revolves around money.

I really get into a story where someone like me, who has the odds stacked against them, takes a risk and wins. And if it's a once-in-a-lifetime opportunity, my adrenaline soars because I fear that if I don't taken action, I'll miss out.

8. Safe Players

I enjoy reading stories that have a happy ending. I want to know that everyone made it home safe and sound. Stories that resonate with me feature people who are cautious about themselves, their money, and their health. I want to be able to participate without feeling like I am going to be burned. I like to see a story that features someone who is a problem solver. I want to know that there is a confident hero in the story, because I will look toward that hero as a role model.

9. Hiding My Compulsion

When I hear stories about individuals who share the same issues that I do, an organization can get my instant attention. I want to know that I am not alone, and I want to see how someone was able to prevail over an issue in their lives. I enjoy the human interest, and knowing there are heroes.

Because I am looking for a hero, I can be drawn deeper inside a message. Story is a big hook to me, and a pathway to my attention. I just want to be like other people. I don't see myself as normal, but I do want to see how I might normalize my life. And I like to see how I can live vicariously through others in the story.

Story is an opportunity for me to build trust in an organization. I've been taken advantage of too many times before, so I must see that I am not going to be taken advantage of again. Allow me to step inside the story, and it will be able to pave deeper grooves for a new memory.

10. Fifty Plus

I love stories. I want to hear about people like myself. I've gone through unique experiences during my lifetime, especially from the decades of the 1960s and 70s. Those were the golden years for baby boomers. I like to hear stories about other people my age and solutions to health concerns, financial pressures, and other concerns that people over the age of 50 can relate to.

I have many concerns weighing on my mind. There are the physical reminders of aging. My children are now young adults, and I worry about how they are going to make it in today's world. But I'm also concerned about aging parents. It's helpful to know how others dealing with similar circumstances are dealing with these pressures.

I am acutely aware that there is no turning back the clock. No story can change that. But I have deeply ingrained memories that make me smile. When I hear a story or read a story from a marketer, it must be relevant to the era in time that I look back on. I want to be led to thinking that there could be a brighter future than what I envision.

11. Business 8 to 5

I don't hear stories very often in business-to-business communications. Yes, I hear testimonials. But stories impact me more. It's tough to break through to score my business. But a story could serve to be influential in how I view and respond to a prospective change from a company where I already do business. I want to hear how another company was able to become more profitable. I realize that most companies don't want to share their results, so I understand that a story can be difficult for a B2B marketer to share. But I would even be interested in listening to a story about how a company was easy to work with and provided great service.

12. Did I Matter?

I enjoy hearing stories about people whose lives have been remembered in a favorable light. This helps to illustrate how others have seen a pathway to fulfilling their life's mission, and how I might be remembered. When I see how someone else's purpose has been enhanced, I go along with the story. It helps me find what I have been searching for my entire life.

I enjoy seeing how others have had emptiness in their heart and mind fulfilled. Uplifting stories take me to a place where I am at peace. It helps me understand that my life really has had purpose and that my values have been fulfilled while I am still alive.

I hate to admit it, but my ego plays a large role in my decisions. Maybe that means I'm a bit insecure, too, but I'm obsessed with knowing that my life has mattered. And stories help affirm me of that possibility for me in the future.

Now let's turn to interpreting your sales message and move closer to closing a sale or generating a contribution.

CHAPTER 9

INTERPRET

After taking your prospect to this place of greater interest in your message, you've already stimulated and calmed emotion, you've presented your unique selling proposition (or positioning), and you've hooked your prospect with a story that amplifies your message, now it's time to begin your close.

YOUR LOGICAL SALES PRESENTATION

There are two parts of the close: interpretation (introducing logic for the metaphorical left brain), and returning your prospect to emotion (in the metaphorical right brain). This chapter will help bring your sales message together by making your logical sales presentation.

The left hemisphere of your brain does, in fact, have more of a logic and mathematical focus. The left and right brain hemispheres are both used when engaging creativity. You might think of this two-part closing as engaging in whole-brain thinking, because you strengthen your message when you appeal to both the left brain and right brain. Using a few formulas, you can advance your message more smoothly toward your objective of generating a lead, sale, or contribution. After the effort to get attention and deliver your message, ultimately it's in the closing where you make your logic-based sales pitch and move your prospective customer back to an emotional place where they give themselves permission to buy, which is the focus of the next chapter.

Your message must interpret the outcome of the story you've told so that your prospect feels as though he or she is in the story. Any skepticism must be put to rest here, including interpretation of features to benefits. Here, you introduce the financial cost, and present it with the perceived return on investment and value component. Solidify your reputation even more through testimonials or reviews of how others have had good experience with your product or organization. You assure the individual, through a strong guarantee, that not only will they be satisfied, but that their lives are transformed to better things.

In any successful content marketing, website, direct mail letter, email, landing page, video or other selling channel, there are certain attributes that enhance the logical side of how people process information. The Greek philosopher Aristotle spoke about ethos, pathos, and logos. Ethos establishes credibility. Pathos persuades the reader through emotional appeals. Logos appeals to a person through reasoning. This sequential process of positioning through logic and emotion is timeless.

A survey by Golin-Harris[33] found that 69 percent of respondents agreed with the statement, "I just don't know who to trust anymore."

Until there is trust, the brain isn't in the proper frame of mind to be fully open to your message. People are skeptical and expect a bad outcome. They reveal less about themselves and are guarded. When that happens, your prospective customer or donor will retreat to protect themselves.

SIX WAYS TO APPEAL TO LOGIC

Through interpretation, you deepen trust. It's the nuance of interpretation—not just throwing out information and letting it sit idly—that's transformational in generating response. Here are six ways to appeal to logic:

1. Features versus Benefits
2. Pricing Presentation
3. Incentives
4. There's More!
5. Testimonials
6. Guarantee

Using these logical appeals can enhance the positivity of your product, service, or organization. Here is more about each of them.

1. Features versus Benefits

It's easy to talk about features of a product or service, but they need to be translated into benefits. You need to spell out why those benefits are important and relevant to your prospective customer.

Often I begin with a checklist, a side-by-side table that enables me to evaluate everything. Using the insurance product example from earlier in this book, here is how a few features and benefits were compared.

Feature: No Medical Exam
Benefit: No embarrassment from an intrusive physical examination
Feature: Premiums locked in for 10 years
Benefit: Even if your health changes, you pay the same amount
Feature: Renewable to age 75 and coverage can't be cancelled
Benefit: Even if your health changes, you are guaranteed to have coverage as long as premiums are paid

With this checklist, I was able to write a promotion that helped transcend the reader from just seeing what the insurance product offered to what it meant to them. After all, every one of us is always wondering, "what's in it for me?"

2. Pricing Presentation

You must sell why your price is fair and reasonable, and how it will deliver a return on its investment. Presenting price can be tricky. You mustn't avoid it. You can't be sneaky. So you need to make sure you don't hit your prospect too hard with the price, but rather ease them into price properly.

Should a marketer lead with price, or wait until the end of the sales presentation after features and benefits have been presented?

There are no absolute answers, and statistically valid A/B testing in a marketing environment will reveal what works for your situation. Still, findings of a study suggest five ways for marketers to disclose price.

This study by neuroscientists and professors from Harvard Business School and Stanford University[34] was conducted to see if considering price first changed the way the brain coded the value of the product.

The research focus was on brain activity when the participant saw price and product presented together. Researchers were most interested in the area in the brain that deals with estimating decision value (the medial prefrontal cortex), and the area of the brain where activity is correlated with whether a product is viscerally desirable. This pleasure center is called the nucleus accumbens.

Fundamentally, the research indicates there are differences in how a person codes information, based on whether the product has a greater emotional attachment, or whether the product was more practical.

They found that brain activity did vary with the sequence of product versus price first. A conclusion of the report is that when the product came first, the decision question seemed to be one of "Do I like it?" When the price came first, the question seemed to be "Is it worth it?" Three other points made in the research suggest that showing price first can make a difference:

- The order of price or product presentation doesn't matter when the product is desirable and easily understood and consumed (e.g., movies, clothes, electronics), and fulfill an emotional need. If the product is affordable in this instance, then it's an easy decision, no matter how price was presented.
- When a product is on sale or bargain-priced, showing price first can positively influence the sale.
- When the product is practical or useful (more than emotional), showing price first prompted participants to be significantly more likely to purchase a product.

"The question isn't whether the price makes a product seem better, it's whether a product is worth its price." said Uma R. Karmarkar, one of the research authors. "Putting the price first just tightens the link between the benefit you get from the price and the benefit you get from the product itself."

For marketers, especially using direct response methods, copywriting formulas often dictate that the price comes toward the end of a sales message, after the product has been presented—particularly in letters and longer-form copy. This study suggests a split test of revealing price first is in order.

If you are going to test revealing price first, here are five positioning ideas:

1. When a product is on sale, prominently show the price. Use dollars, not percentages. Percentages aren't easily interpreted in the mind (or worse, they are miscalculated in the mind and you risk losing a sale).
2. Incrementally break down the price. Show it as the cost per day, cost per use, or some other practical way to reveal price increments.
3. Compare price to an everyday item. One of my most successful direct mail packages included a letter with a headline that said, "For about the cost of a cup of coffee a day, you can have…"
4. Compare to your competition. If you have a price advantage, show it. If you don't, then compare at different levels that includes longer product life, more convenience, or other benefits.
5. Position the price presentation as a cost of not buying now. In other words, show how the price could increase in the future, or the loss that can happen by waiting. This positioning also creates urgency.

Importantly, the research didn't study emotion-based long-copy with storytelling and unique selling positioning of the product. Using emotion, story, and a strong USP before revealing price may be more effective to sell your product. Every situation is different. The only way to conclusively know if revealing price first will generate a higher response than presenting the sales message first is to split test, across small, statistically significant circulation quantities of each version.

3. Incentives
When you sweeten the deal, you appeal to logic. More importantly, buyers expect something extra. It's cultural.

Why do incentives work in selling? It's because consumers are confronted daily with a barrage of offers. For some consumers, the barrage is so overwhelming they shut down. So, as you think about an add-on deal, consider that the incentive needs to logically flow from your core offer. A few ideas can include:

- Special pricing.
- Free shipping.
- Discount to purchase multiple items.
- An extra report or information product of high perceived value.
- Fast response bonus.

Consider, too, how you can "pile on" multiple incentives. This is a strategy that helps your prospective customer to feel like they are getting a lot of extras. One of these techniques is the "false close."

4. "But Wait! There's More!"

If you've watched infomercials on television, you've seen (or certainly have heard about) ads that feature a classic line, "But wait, there's more!" That declaration is called a false close. The concept (not those exact words) is proven to work in direct mail, too, usually in long-form letter copy.

This is a concept I first learned about from American Writers and Artists (awaionline.com).[35] AWAI, in my opinion, is the premier copywriting training program for direct response copywriters. I've spoken at their events and teach online courses for them from time-to-time.

The false close is a concept that can be used in most selling scenarios because it's really nothing more than a technique to surprise and delight the buyer. By this point in the sales pitch, you've emotionally hooked the prospective buyer. In fact, you might be able ask for the sale and get it.

With the false close, you're able to add another benefit that's extra and wasn't expected. The bonus for you is that this technique sets up the customer to feel even better about the decision to purchase.

There are two aspects of the false close: you approach as if you're going to ask for the sale, then you withdraw, taking your prospect in a different direction.

The approach should only be taken after the sales message has been adequately presented. You act like you're going to close the sale, then you do what your prospect least expects: you withdraw. What you achieve is lowering resistance by doing something unpredictable. Then you add another promise or benefit. When you do this, you aren't so predictable and your message is fresh and more interesting.

In the approach phase you have finished your successful sales presentation. You remind your prospect of your promise and major benefits. Then in the withdrawal you can surprise your prospect. You can mention added benefits: premiums, free gifts, or other considerations such as free shipping. Chances are you have seen some of these withdrawal examples:

- "By the way there is one more thing I forgot to tell you…"
- "Before I give you all the details let me quickly tell you about yet another unusual idea I'm excited about right now…"
- "There's one more important thing I'd like to tell you about …"

5. Testimonials

Your prospective customers want to hear what credible people who are just like them have to say about your product, service or organization.

Your best testimonials are organic. That is, they are unsolicited and come into a customer service department. All too often customer service departments do a poor job of making sure those testimonials are shared with the marketing department. Make sure you have implemented a procedure for your customer service staff to distribute those testimonials and letters. They are gold to the selling process. Remember, too, when you get a testimonial to ask your customer for permission (in writing) to use their testimonial. Get a photo of them if you can.

A "pull quote," (that is, a short portion) lifted from a long testimonial letter should be included in both printed and online marketing messaging. If you can, encourage your customer to get out a video camera or smartphone and record themselves saying great things about your organization.

6. Guarantee

Your guarantee is a vital part of your success. You might think of it as a promise to have money returned if a buyer isn't satisfied. While that's true, that is really only a superficial use.

There is so much more to a guarantee than what many marketers realize. It's an opportunity for you to solidify a relationship and resolve any lingering doubts. You see, by this point in the selling process there are inevitably doubts starting to creep in to the mind. This is where you can reassure your prospect.

A word about the graphic treatment of your guarantee: an official-looking border will give your guarantee more visual credibility. Using a spiral border or ornate-looking design, like a certificate, will give instant visual cues of security and credibility, to your prospective customer.

Use these six ways to appeal to logic, and you'll succeed in interpreting your offer.

NUMERIC SPEED BUMPS

Your prospects are moving fast these days in an "always-on" world. Fast thinking normally trumps slow thinking, yet sometimes you need to slow down thinking long enough to convert your prospect into a paying customer. Your most challenging task may be slowing down your prospective customers just enough that they don't skip over your sales message.

Fast thinking is always set to the "on" position. Fast thinking is instinctive and automatic. Whatever pops into the mind of your prospect often happens with no conscious control, and sometimes fast thinking works in your favor with a quick, impulsive decision to buy.

But, not always.

As you set out to grab attention during these frenzied times, remember that when the mind is in fast thinking mode, short, simple sentences with smaller words are more effective. Content that's breezy in style usually prevails over hard-to-read copy.

How do you get the fast thinker to slow down when you want them to make a decision?

Here's where you can create speed bumps in your message, so the mind doesn't slide down its established memory grooves too quickly and pass you by.

One way to get attention is by introducing numbers. Numbers—especially dollars and cents—are effective speed bumps.

For people to respond to numeric data effectively, they need to be able to do three things:

1. Comprehend the number.
2. Interpret it in proper context.
3. Act on it.

For example, when our daughters were small children, one of the ways that I discovered how to get them out of an emotional tantrum was to ask a question requiring a numerical answer. Questions like "how old are you?" or "how old will you be on your next birthday?" worked like a charm to move our kids from their right brain emotional state to a left brain logical state and slow down their impulsive thinking.

So, when using numbers in marketing copy, you can slow down the readers' thinking with these five speed bumps, which include some of the pricing suggestions from earlier in this chapter:

1. Ask a question that requires a numeric answer.
2. Reveal pricing in small chunks, such as a cost per day.
3. Display discounts in dollars, not percentages. Not everyone quickly grasps that 30% off a $100.00 item equals $30.00. Better to say "save $30.00."
4. Illustrate the rate of improvement or satisfaction gains using specific numbers. Better: give numbers visual life in charts or graphs.
5. Guarantee your product or service for a specific number of days (more time, such as 60 or 90, is stronger than 30 days).

All that being said, you may be able to get a prospect to make a purchase decision in your favor from snap thinking and decision-making (and if you can close them quickly, then why not?). Most people don't act that impulsively. Impulsive decisions are a slippery slope on the way to buyer's remorse. Slow them down, if you can, with a few strategically placed speed bumps.

READING-LEVEL APPROPRIATE COPY

When was the last time you checked your copy's grade level reading scores? Now that you've presented your logical sales message, it's time to check if your content has been written at the most optimal grade-level for your audience.

The reading level of Americans is declining, and you could be writing over your prospective customer's ability to understand your message. In the U.S., average reading levels are at about the 8th grade level. But 1-in-5 U.S. adults read below a 5th grade level. And surprisingly, 14% of U.S. adults can't read, according to the U.S. Department of Education, National Institute of Literacy.[36]

Grade levels at which high school students are reading have dropped. It's now at 5th grade levels,[37] and is an ominous sign for the future.

Even the writing and delivery of recent Presidential State of the Union addresses are at lower grade levels[38] than in generations past. President George H.W. Bush averaged a reading level of 8.6. Barack Obama averaged 9.4. Bill Clinton, 9.8. George W. Bush, 10.0. Compare these scores to over fifty years ago with Dwight Eisenhower at 12.6 and John F. Kennedy at 12.3.

Given these declining readability statistics, chances are that your copy is written above the reading ability and comprehension of your prospects and customers.

So what to do?

Three tips:

1. **Know Your Audience.** Using your persona, you'll have a sense of this market's reading ability.
2. **Research and Test.** Conduct research and examine your copy to identify the reading level of your audience. For reference, *TV Guide* and *Reader's Digest* are written at the 9th grade, and *USA Today* at a 10th grade level.
3. **Flesch–Kincaid Reading Ease and Grade Level Test.** Use the Flesch–Kincaid Reading Ease and Grade Level test in Microsoft Word. Go

to "Review," "Spelling & Grammar," and after you spell check your document, you'll see readability statistics. You'll see the number of sentences per paragraph, words per sentence, characters per word, percent passive sentences, Flesch Reading Ease (the higher the better) and ultimately, your Flesch-Kincaid Grade Level score (lower is usually better, depending on your audience).

For passive sentences, a lower ranking is better than higher. Target 10% or less. The passive voice is not as interesting and exciting as the active voice.

If the Reading Ease Score is lower than you want, and the Grade Level score is higher than you want, isolate paragraphs and sentences to identify problematic copy. Here's how you change the score:

- Use smaller words.
- Shorten sentences.
- Shorten paragraphs.

A review of your copy's Reading Ease and Grade Level is an essential step that should be automatic every time you write and evaluate copy. A score that is reflective of your audience can lead to better comprehension, leading to more sales.

INTERPRETING FOR THE 12 PERSONAS

Now that you've been given insights into how you should form your logical sales message, let's return to the personas for their inner thoughts about they interpret information.

1. Trailblazers/Early Adopters

I'm usually a few steps ahead of most people, so I've got things figured out before the marketer does. Tell me if you think you must, but I can figure out the benefits. I like features and bright shiny objects. You see, I expect there will be no issues with a product. I expect superiority and quality. So you'd better have credible arguments in place that takes me to that logical place in my mind.

Listen, I'm not all that concerned about price. I'll pay what I think it's worth, and I'll pay a premium if the situation is right. Still, I like to feel like I got a good deal, even if the seller threw in a little "gimme" with enough value that I can brag about getting something for nothing.

I do want to see a guarantee, but spare me the nonsense and just tell me that you stand behind your product.

2. My Brand/My Lifestyle/My Growth

Even though I have been given a good positioning and storyline about a product, I like to have it interpreted so I can see how it can impact me. I want to know that the outward aesthetics will cultivate an attitude for me that will make me feel better about myself.

I also want a guarantee that is less about numbers and more about feeling. This is all about what a product or service will do for me. Price is a consideration, but I'm less concerned about price as long as I see a benefit in purchasing a product. Value is most important to me even if the price point is hefty. I will make it work for me if I see the value of it, but you will have to show me how the price point makes sense and delivers on what will make me feel better about myself.

3. Money Matters

Interpretation of product features and benefits are very important to me. I need a considerable amount of logic in the sales message to take me to a place where I will consider responding. I like details. But I also need those details translated into benefits. Those can be the tipping points for me.

Prices need to be explained to me in a way that shows value. I like to see pricing broken down into ways such as price per day, price per unit, or the long-term value of a product after time. I've got to be sold.

A strong guarantee is essential for me. A guarantee that is specific and is stated in long-term value, such as 90 days versus 30 days, means a lot. When you present me with a 30-day guarantee, my mental clock starts ticking so that as I approached the 30th day, it creates uncertainty for me and I wonder if I should return the product. More time is better.

4. On Financial Edge

While it's important for me to understand all of the details, I admit that I don't always pay a lot of attention to them. Sometimes I barely understand them. I just want a solution for what's most important to me right now. It's hard for me to think very far into the future. I want to know how a product or organization can help me at this moment, not next month.

Since I'm not very good with details, I just need to have the one, two, or three most important things that I can understand spelled out for me. Don't make this complicated, if you do, I'll have to pass on it because if I can't understand it then I can't act on it.

5. Right Thing to Do: Taking the High Road

Because I believe in doing the right thing, information needs to be interpreted for me so that I can clearly see that an organization supports my beliefs. There can be no issues with any product or service. Any logic in the interpretation of a product's offer must serve an important purpose so that I can see it supports my point of view.

I take a logical approach to my thinking, so a logical argument that can be built for me enables me to trust in the interpretation. A guarantee needs to go beyond price and time value. It needs to go to the heart of my attitude where I feel gratified that I have made the right choice. I don't tend to get over consumed with cost. I recognize the extra price is sometimes what it takes to support my belief system and values.

6. Love and Social Relationships

I like to understand how making a decision will positively influence my life. I don't need a lot of logical explanation, but I do need some. I need to understand benefits, pricing, and a guarantee. I'd love to read about a guarantee that says I will never have rejection again in my life. Not realistic, but that's what I would like to see.

I don't want to say that price is no object, but if I can clearly see how a product will work for me and the price and the benefits make sense, I will make an emotional decision to move forward.

Both features and benefits are essential for me to understand. Benefits need to illustrate how I am going to feel whole in my relationships.

7. Adrenaline Seekers: Opportunists

Even though my adrenaline makes me highly emotional, I still like to have a logical argument. I'm a bit torn between logic and emotion. The adrenaline junkie side of me wants to instinctively act without significant heaps of logic. Yet I can be taken down a path through a story that builds to a logical argument and draws me in. It helps me rationalize my decision-making.

I want to be guaranteed that I have the opportunity reserved for myself. For me, money is useful to bringing me enjoyment. If I think I can beat the system, I don't object to paying a price. But the price needs to be logically spelled out for me.

8. Safe Players

By nature, I am a logical person. That means that any marketing message needs to be persuasive in a way that lays out all of the arguments in a logical sequence. A guarantee is vital for me to see. I never want to feel like I have been burned by overpaying. I must feel comfortable with an offer.

Benefits trump features for me. The benefits must be very clear and flow from the big picture all the way to the details so that I can see multiple parts of the story. The offer must include the safety and security that I require before I make a purchase.

Because I am a bit more pessimistic than optimistic, a marketing message must logically flow so that it aligns with my thought process. I am doubtful of my decisions. But when I find a marketer who helps me solve problems through logical arguments, I am more apt to do business with them.

9. Hiding My Compulsion

I tend to be more emotional than logical. Once I have gained trust and feel that my boundaries will be respected, I will listen. So an organization must interpret features into benefits that are sensitive to my emotions. For me, logic can be best communicated as part of the story. I must be guaranteed safety and confidentiality. A guarantee that is filled with numbers and logic is less persuasive to me than one that is more emotional in tone.

Interpreting price points isn't terribly important. I am so heavily driven by my emotion that a price of a product or service pales in comparison to the benefit that I feel I will receive. That's why for a marketer's logic they must build on benefits upon benefits so that price is not a significant consideration.

10. Fifty Plus

There is so much noise and a bombardment of information and choices that the interpretation of information must go to my heart. I'm over the age of 50, and at a different point in my life. It's a place I've never known or experienced before. I need complex information explained to me.

Logical arguments from my peers are more credible to me. I'm also beginning to listen to the logical arguments of generations older than me. As baby boomers, we didn't always trust those who are older than us. We were the ones, after all, who were leading a new charge in the culture of the world. But now that I am aging, I appreciate and respect what people who are younger than me are saying about those who are older. The millennial generation, represented by my children, is beginning to become a stronger influence in my life.

The changing economy has been difficult for me. As technology rapidly changes around me, I'm not always as quick to adapt it. I look to younger people who can help me, so I want to hear from an organization who understands that dynamic.

I'm also entering a point in my life where I am more price sensitive than I used to be. Economic challenges in recent years have stripped away money. I feel I've lost time in saving for retirement. My confidence to spend money isn't as high as it once was. I must see a logical argument that will show endurance of product. I need to know it will last long or that it will significantly improve my life.

Guarantees are important to me. I've seen too many points of disruption in recent years and I'm worried that things will change greatly in the future.

11. Business 8 to 5

It's important that I see features and benefits side-by-side. I need to be able to see those comparisons so that I can make an objective decision. If something goes wrong in a new business relationship, I will want to point at evidence that gets me off the hook. I can't have all eyes and the blame on me if a decision goes badly.

I want to see a strong guarantee. I need to have promised features put in writing. I will need to read your agreement and have any contracts approved.

Pricing is important to understand. I am most annoyed when I am promised one price but then delivered another. When I'm comparison shopping, one thing that really irritates me is how companies provide quotes that are confusing and inconsistent with how others price their products or services. Transparency in pricing is important.

12. Did I Matter?

I'm a logical person. I want to understand step-by-step how my money is used today, and how I am going to be remembered. I like to see organizations recognize that they understand my life's purpose. I want to see that my dreams and goals are put into action.

I want to understand how I am going to be remembered. And since I don't always know myself how I want to be remembered, it's helpful to be given illustrations of how that might look. I want to be convinced that there will be long-lasting goodwill created because of the choices that I make now.

This is a significant emotional decision for me. I understand that there can be no guarantee that I will be remembered forever, but I want assurances that steps will be taken so that I will be remembered for a long time to come.

Now let's take your customer back to the heart and emotion and enable permission to act.

CHAPTER 10

PERMISSION TO ACT

This is where you close your sale. You have stirred your prospect's emotion, calmed their mind, positioned your product properly, and told the story to create new memory. You moved them to the logical part of your sales message, and now it's time to seize the moment and bring them back to the emotional side of their thinking so that they allow themselves permission to act.

OPEN THE DOOR TO PERMISSION

This is where your message should naturally lead the individual to say to themselves, "this is good, this is smart for me, and I give myself permission to act, buy, or contribute now."

It's important to reinforce that no one can force any other person into a decision. You must lead your prospect to a place where they want to inquire, buy or donate. Think about yourself: have you ever been forced to act? No. You dig your heals in. Rather, you've made purchase decisions, after concluding that making that decision was in your best interest. So it is with converting your prospect into a paying (or donating) customer.

When you've made your logical left brain appeal, you must move your reader to the emotional right brain. Bring your prospect to becoming a customer with these conclusions:

Persona

Stimulate

Calm

Position

Story

Interpret

Permission

- **This is Good.** You must lead your audience to conclude that "this is good" about your offer.

- **This is Smart.** If it's good and you've done your job correctly as you interpreted your sales proposition, then your prospect can think to themselves that "this is smart for me."

- **Open the Door to Permission to Act.** In the closing of your message, lead your prospect logically and emotionally to a place where in their mind they give themselves permission to buy.

HOW TO NEUTRALIZE BACKFIRE

As you are getting closer to sealing the deal, consider that there is always a risk of your message backfiring. The backfire effect can blow up in your face, no matter what you're selling.

Attempting to change someone's belief is a tall task. It's true of you, and it's true of your prospects. As people age and accumulate more information, and the memory grooves in the mind become more deeply etched, it is more difficult to change a mind.

Though it may sound ridiculous to defend beliefs even when they are proved inaccurate, there are several examples to illustrate it. For instance, there are people who still disagree that the Holocaust happened. Some deniers are misled, while others deny the genocide for racist, political, or strategic reasons. The event itself was unprecedented, irrational, and inconceivable.

Yet, a myriad of sources prove that the Holocaust happened. Further, experiments and historical examples also prove that humans can hurt one another.

Consider these external factors that, as a marketer, you can't alter:

- The human mind will instinctively and unconsciously resist change. Once something is added to a belief system, it is defended from change.

- When presented with information that is inconsistent with a belief system, beware of the backfire effect. It happens when an individual is defending information that they are seeking. Oftentimes, people seek information that simply reinforces their original thinking.

- Some people stick to beliefs no matter what. It doesn't matter if there are facts refuting a position with an avalanche of data pointing to an obvious alternative conclusion. Some people will not change their mind.

Keeping these external factors in mind is essential for marketers. Knowing them enables you to craft content that can be more accepted. When writing copy, remember, you are trying to create new memory grooves in the mind. One approach to overcome disagreement is to cite facts and figures, but when someone vehemently disagrees, you risk making someone feel stronger about their position. Your sales message can backfire. Worse, your prospect may push deeper into an entrenched belief system.

It's more challenging when your prospects are confronted with something counter to their beliefs. They often respond by seeking out information that supports their already-established memory, even if the information is inaccurate. The unintended result: It grooves their memory even more deeply.

Today, easy Internet access adds even more fuel to this backfire, or pushback. As people selectively seek out information that supports their belief—even if it's factually wrong—the inaccurate belief can be bolstered by inaccurate claims. Look at newsfeeds on social media. Every minute on the wild web of social media, people are reposting one-sided stories that support a particular belief, accepting it as proof.

So what can you do to reduce the risk of the backfire effect as you move closer to a sale? Consider these approaches when presenting your sales message:

- **Know the Persona**. Yes, we're back to the persona and for good reason. Before you write your sales message, know the persona of your intended market or audience. A well-conceived persona will reveal what your prospect most likely thinks so that you avoid the land mine of the backfire effect.
- **Approach the Underlying Emotion First**. Begin by gaining trust within an existing belief system. If you need to change your prospect's mind, do it by understanding the underlying emotion of your prospect first, and gain empathy.

- **Use a Simple Positioning**. Your prospect is more apt to follow your thought process with explanations that take little effort to process. Keep your positioning short and simple.
- **Use a Story**. Allow your reader to see themselves inside a story that makes a point and leads to a specific conclusion.
- **Close with Emotion**. Start with emotion, build your logical case (ethos), and then close with an emotional appeal (pathos). Emotion usually prevails over logic, even when the logic is flawed.

Coming full circle, these ideas about how to approach each persona can help you make the sale. Bring your prospective customer back to an emotional place, and let them give themselves permission to act when you have convinced them that acting is good and it's smart for them.

- **Command Undivided Attention.** If you want your prospective customer's undivided attention, get it through activating fear.
- **Encourage Thinking.** Once you have undivided attention, take quick advantage of it by encouraging your prospect to pause and think.
- **Be the Problem Solver.** Your prospect wants easy and quick solutions, especially in a media multitasking world. You can become their virtual problem solver.
- **Organize Yourself First So You Can Organize Them.** When attention is split apart, you must do the heavy lifting of organizing your message and quickly deliver it with clarity. Confusion kills interest.
- **Relieve Anxiety.** You can be the salvation in your prospect's life to relieve anxiety. Be credible. Solve problems. Be your prospect's hero.

Remember, too, that oftentimes our prospects and customers make decisions and respond based on intuition, a hunch, or professional judgment. It's at this point that gut reaction can turn the prospect away and leave you empty handed.

HEADING OFF GUT REACTION THAT CAN PREVAIL AND DERAIL

In marketing and sales, we instinctively want quick action. We know that if the prospect drifts away from our message, we'll lose them, usually forever. So while the logic and quantification of your sales story may be overwhelmingly in your favor, the prospect's intuition can turn them away. This is because of something that felt too good to be true, leaves room for skepticism, or an unintended nuance in copy that you overlooked loses the sale for you.

Even if all the arguments you've made in your content are authentically and credibly in your favor, a person's gut decision often prevails.

But here's what is frustrating: often a person's gut reaction is wrong because it's subject to bias. Your prospect might overestimate his ability to assemble a product, for example. He or she may think it takes too much time to read your information, learning materials, or book. Perhaps when your prospect has made a mistake related to what you're selling, he doesn't understand why, or is hesitant to ask for help or feedback. He forgets. That is, he forgot the last time he made a poor decision based on his gut instead of listening to logic.

How do you overcome gut emotion and reaction? You have to help your prospective customers or donors through the decision making process. Do it with these ideas:

- **Lead Your Prospect to a Sense of Revelation**. That happens when your conscious mind finally learns something that your subconscious mind already knew. Ask yourself: when are you most creative (what you might consider right brain thinking)? For most people, it's during exercise, walking, jogging, listening to music, in the shower, or in an unfamiliar environment. Some of my best ideas have struck me while on vacation, when my mind is suspended from the consciousness of day-to-day responsibilities. Lead your prospect to an awakening that feels like it has come from within.
- **Give 'em Chills and Goosebumps.** A reaction inside the mind often is accompanied by a physical sensation. It could be chills or goosebumps. For some people, it may be an unusual feeling in the stomach or throat.

You can create these physical sensations when copy is accompanied by strong visuals that paint a picture, or when a video or website has powerful music or images.

- **Past Experience Recall.** Your brain's hippocampus stores long-term memory. Long-term memories are with you for your entire life, unless something comes along to establish new grooves and create a new memory. You aren't likely to replace past long-term memories, but you do have the opportunity to either create another memory that neutralizes a bad memory or enhances a good one. Creating new memory is harder to do than drawing on a past memory. When you can, allow your content to take your prospect to a positive place, or hit a negative memory head-on with a turnaround story or illustration so strong you can overcome the negativity.

- **Challenge The Perceptual Rules Made Up in the Mind.** For some people, changing an ingrained rule is impossible, even if it's wrong. When a person can't articulate why the rule exists, you may be able to use an overwhelming amount of empirical data or statistics from credible third party sources to turn around a rules-based individual. But don't count on it.

- **Recognize Patterns and Cross-Index.** Help your prospect see something familiar to engage intuitive skills. The more material about your product or service that you can provide to cross-index in the mind, the higher likelihood your prospect's intuition will kick in on a positive note.

You won't always be able to prevail over intuition or gut reaction, but when you anticipate that probability in your copy, you can turn around a potential lost sale.

PRINCIPLES OF PERSUASION

So you've created your campaign and attended to all the details of identifying your audience, created your offer, and toiled for hours and hours, honing copywriting and design. As you approach the final stages of getting the desired response, the tipping point for your success likely stems from the degree to which you emotionally persuade an individual to take action.

Persuasion builds. It doesn't just pop up and present itself. To seal the deal, with your return to emotion, you still need to persuade.

Persuasion is an art, really, that builds over time. It's earning trust and leading your prospect to a place where they give themselves permission to act. That permission comes from the individual recognizing that acting is in their interest and that they will feel good about their decision to say "this is good, this is smart, I'm going to do this!"

A place to start this list of persuasion points is with the six principles from the landmark book, *Influence: How and Why People Agree to Things*, by Robert Cialdini:[39]

- Reciprocity
- Commitment and Consistency
- Social Proof
- Liking
- Authority
- Scarcity

Expanding on Cialdini's concepts with additional principles for marketers, I offer this checklist for persuasion:

1. **Trust and Credibility**. Persuasion isn't coercion or manipulation. Trust is earned. Credibility is built. Without these two foundational elements, most else won't matter. Begin persuading by building trust and credibility first.

2. **Authority.** People respect authority figures. The power of authority commands respect and burrows deep into the mind. Establish your organization, a spokesperson, or an everyday person, relatable to your customer, as having authority.

3. **Express Interest.** Your prospects are attracted to organizations that have an interest in them. Use this starter list of "Seven F's" as central topics

to build around so you can persuade by expressing interest: Family, Friends, Fun, Food, Fashion, Fitness, or Fido/Felines.

4. **Build Desire for Gain.** A major motivation that persuades your prospects and customers is the desire for gain. Give your prospect more of the things they value in life, such as more money, success, health, respect, influence, love and happiness.

5. **Simplify and Clarify.** Communicate clearly. Obsess over simplifying the complex. Write to the appropriate grade level of your reader. Your prospects are more easily persuaded when you simplify and clarify.

6. **Expose Deep Truths.** Go deeper with your persuasive message by telling your prospects things about themselves that others aren't saying. Don't be judgmental. Be respectful.

7. **Commitment and Consistency.** When your prospect commits to your idea, they will honor that commitment because the idea was compatible with their self-image. Compatibility opens the door to persuasion.

8. **Social Proof.** Even though the first edition of Cialdini's book was written in 1984, a generation before the explosion of social media, he recognized the power of people behaving with a "safety in numbers" attitude from seeing what other people were doing. Testimonials and an active and positive presence on social media are often a must that leads to trust and persuasion.

9. **Liking.** The term "liking" in 1984 was developed in the context of people being persuaded by those they like. People are persuaded and more apt to buy if they like the individual or organization. Still, it's affirming to be "liked" on social media.

10. **Confidence is Contagious.** When you convey your unwavering belief in what your product or organization can do for your prospect, that attitude persuades and will come through loud and clear.

11. **Reciprocity.** It is human nature for us to return a favor and treat others as they treat us. Gestures of giving something away as part of your offer can set you up so that your prospects are persuaded and happy to give you something in return: their business.

12. **Infuse Energy.** People are drawn toward, and persuaded by, being invigorated and motivated. Infuse energy in your message.

13. **Remind about Fear of Loss.** No matter how much a person already possesses, most want more. People naturally possess the fear of missing out (FOMO). When you include them, they are more easily persuaded.

14. **Guarantee.** Your guarantee should transcend more than the usual "satisfaction or your money back." Your guarantee can persuade through breaking down sales resistance and solidify a relationship.

15. **Scarcity.** Human nature desires to possess things that are scarce when we fear losing out on an offer presented with favorable terms. Make sure you honor the positioning of scarcity in your message. If it's an offer not to be repeated, don't repeat it.

16. **Convey Urgency.** With scarcity comes urgency. Offering your product or making a special bonus available for a "limited time" with a specific deadline can be a final tipping point to persuade.

17. **Tenacity and Timing.** Just because a prospect said "no" the first, second or more times, it doesn't mean you should give up on someone who is in your audience. It can take multiple points of contact, from multiple channels, before you persuade your prospect to give themselves permission to act.

GIVING PERMISSION TO ACT FOR THE 12 PERSONAS

Now that you're at the crucial place of opening up the mind so the prospective customer or donor takes action, here are ways different personas are apt to give themselves the permission to act.

1. Trailblazers/Early Adopters

Here's what motivates me to act: Knowing a product is for real, it's new and advanced, and that I'm going to be the first to have it!

If I can recall a past experience that gave me great pleasure, and proved to myself once again that I'm an innovator, I'll give myself permission to act. I use my gut instinct to make a decision, but when I know it's right, I'll freely give myself permission to buy it now.

2. My Brand/My Lifestyle/My Growth

I have to admit that my purchase decisions are usually based on the emotion that I feel at the time. It's a part of my instinct. It's a part of my decision of whether it will advance my brand, lifestyle or personal growth. I need to visually see and instinctively feel when an offer is right for me. I need to be able to step into the offer and see how it will fit with me for my lifestyle choices. When that happens, I will feel a chill that instinctively tells me that I can now give myself permission to purchase.

Past memories are very strong for me. I remember when I was given compliments in the past, and they made me feel great. That's the power of a new look and a new brand. That's the emotion I must feel to give myself permission to act.

3. Money Matters

I sense chills when I see a great value for my money. This is what it takes to go to an emotional place where I feel I can give myself permission to act.

Because I am so pragmatic, I enjoy accumulation of possessions only when it makes sense in my life.

Past memories are strong motivators for me. When I am taken back to something that gave me great joy that I still enjoy today, and was a great value, I'm reminded that it was a smart decision at the time. I like to logically and emotionally conclude that a decision is right for me. I must be taken to a place where I say to myself, "This is smart, this is good, and I give myself permission to act."

4. On Financial Edge

I give myself permission to act if I can see that this is a product that's going to help me right now. I need to know that it's accessible to me. I need to know that I'm not going to be burned or otherwise regret my decision. I'll even take a chance sometimes if I'm uncertain.

Some days are desperate for me. Make it easy, understandable, and accessible right now. I don't want any hassle. If it seems like it's in my best interest, I will quickly make a decision to act.

5. Right Thing to Do: Taking the High Road

I sense a feeling of peace when I make a decision to act because I see it supports my belief system. I simply cannot have any apprehension that my decision is anything less than the right thing to do. Sometimes a tipping point for me is within an offer such as a bonus or doing something good for a cause I support.

When I recall a past positive experience that supports and reinforces my belief, my mind opens. I get chills and feel a physiological reaction whenever I do something that supports my belief system. By releasing myself from skepticism I give myself permission to act.

6. Love and Social Relationships

As a naturally emotional person, I like to recall fond memories of the past. Whenever those times occur, I feel emptiness. I want to feel like I am going to be fulfilled. Past memory recall is a strong motivator for me, but I have both negative and positive recollections. If I feel negative, I may not be moved to take action. But if I feel positive, especially if I feel a revelation of what something will do to strengthen love and social relationships, I will be inclined to give myself permission to act.

Let me feel chills and I will be pushed over the edge. This is where I conclude that a decision is right for me.

7. Adrenaline Seekers: Opportunists

I feel chills when I'm emotionally taken to a place where my adrenaline takes over. When that happens, I simply give myself permission to impulsively act. But I want to feel that an organization has my best interest in mind. That's where I say to myself, "This is good, this is smart, and I give myself the permission required to respond."

When I see a pattern of my past behavior that I've benefited from, I'm especially drawn to act. I will instinctively feel when it's the right decision for me, and when I do, I'll make a quick decision. Chills are important to me. That's when I know my adrenaline is pumping, and it's what drives me to make decisions.

8. Safe Players

I'm not an individual who feels chills very often. It's probably a slow process to gain my trust and comfort before I give myself permission to act. Ultimately, I have to feel comfortable and secure before making a decision.

I recognize past opportunities that have worked well for me. I'm highly intuitive. For that reason, an organization has to be careful not to repulse me or turn me off by provoking the wrong gut reaction. I need an organization who will work with me to fix any challenges in my perceptions.

I have to be slowly taken to a point where I realize that the marketer's offer is good and smart for me. That means marketers are going to have to work harder to get me to act. But once I trust a marketer, I will be a customer for a very long time, because for me, it's all about safety and security.

9. Hiding My Compulsion

It can take time to bring me to a tipping point where I come to the conclusion that an organization has my best interests at heart. They'll have to work with me. I have been hurt so many times in my life that I instinctively believe that I'm not going to benefit from an offer. Past memory recall is very strong for me, so a marketer must make a strong, credible point in order to succeed in paving new grooves in my memory. When I feel that, I will know it is time for me to act. That happens after trust has been delivered and I am confident that I will never be betrayed.

10. Fifty Plus

I have had so many different life experiences that I'm weary. When I'm taken to a place about something in my sub conscious mind, I realize some of the things that I should be doing now. I know that I should be saving for my financial future. I know that I should be eating healthy food and exercising to doing better things for my health. There are so many complex issues as a person ages. I'd like to hide those thoughts and think that those realities don't exist. So a marketer needs to bring it forward in my mind and take me to a place where I have to give myself permission to act.

Enable me to feel youthful again and invoke a pleasant past memory. Show me how that past and pleasant memory in my life will benefit me now. I have many perceptions that have been built over many years of my life. Some of those must be overcome. When that happens, I will feel chills. Then I can conclude on my own that "this is good, this is smart, and I will give myself permission to act."

11. Business 8 to 5

It takes a quite a bit to move me to the tipping point of making a decision to respond. I'll need to proceed one step at a time. It probably means that I'm going to initially ask the vendor for some basic information so that I can start research. That's pretty easy. But I don't want to feel like I'm opening myself up to being hounded by a salesperson.

If a company has built my trust in them, I'm more apt to give myself permission to act, even if it's just to inquire. But I may need to have several conversations that lead to a purchase decision. It may be a process. But ultimately what will take me to a point to give myself the permission to either endorse, support, or outright make a purchase decision will be my confidence that they can deliver and that there will be no surprises.

12. Did I Matter?

Before I will give myself permission to contribute to a cause where I can be remembered, I need to be awakened with overwhelming emotion. When that happens, I will feel goosebumps and chills. A tipping point can be if I feel that I will be taken from obscurity to fame.

When pleasant memories of the past can be invoked, it helps to symbolize who I was in my lifetime, and demonstrate that whatever an organization offers will provide a form of legacy for me. I want to know that whatever my choices, this is going to be good and smart for me, and good and smart for future generations.

CHAPTER 11

MIND PATHWAY COMPREHENSION BY CHANNEL

You've seen the proclamations over the years that print channels are near death, along with the counter-arguments that it's nowhere near dead. Here is a deeper perspective of the reason why print won't die. It's as simple as comprehension. Research reveals comprehension is better when information is consumed in print. And there's more: millennials—digital natives, if you prefer—prefer print.[40]

Count me among those who prefer to read the news from a printed newspaper rather than my iPad. Books? My concentration is pitiful if I try to read an e-book. Still, I do a lot of reading—or maybe it's more like scanning—online. I realize there are others of all ages who feel they comprehend content on electronic devices just fine. Or who at least think they comprehend the content. Research published at Academia.com[41] reports how students only think they comprehend as well on digital devices (the research suggests they don't).

One might think that jumping from reading on printed pages to reading on a digital screen is a no-brainer. But biologically, reading has been an evolutionary development over hundreds—even thousands—of years, as suggested in an article in Scientific American.[42]

Our brains evolved to keep the human species alive, eat, and reproduce as you read earlier in this book. Reading is a new addition to the mind, biologically speaking. It took unimaginable centuries for the brain to adapt to reading text in print. And now, in just a generation or so, the human race has been introduced to reading on screens, another reading adaption for the mind.

As a marketer, you need to recognize which channels are best suited for reading comprehension, and how you can effectively create Short- or Long-Term Memory that persuasively leads to a sale.

THREE STAGES OF COMPREHENSION

As I see it, there are three stages of comprehension:

1. **Glance and Forget** in seconds what people just saw or read (the vast majority of what happens with marketing and advertising messages).
2. **Short-Term Reading Comprehension** that evaporates in just minutes or hours.
3. **Long-Term Memory Comprehension** that can last several hours, a day, maybe a week, and in a few instances, a lifetime.

People can only stuff so much into the mind and memory. There is a place for "Glance and Forget" channels when multiple instances of "Glance and Forget" impressions build over time to create awareness and anticipation. When you want your marketing efforts to convert to a sale, you need at least the "Short-Term Reading Comprehension" stage. The most successful campaigns, I believe, will make it to the most valuable "Long-Term Memory Comprehension" stage when the seven pathways of the mind are used.

Digital and print channels can co-exist and strengthen each other. Digital is useful for the moment when a person is looking for top-line or summary information, or just a place to make a quick impression (recognizing there is an additive effect of impressions over time). Print is most useful and effective when your prospect is ready to pause, read and more deeply comprehend, leading to long-term memory and action.

COMPREHENSION BY CHANNEL

My experience suggests that marketers can best leverage certain channels in these ways:

- **Social Media.** Serve readers short, light content. Build your brand, organization and follower base. Don't expect action beyond likes and shares (which you can't take to the bank). But social media, in my experience, is good for positive impressions and building top-of-mind awareness. Keep it curious, likeable and sharable. But don't expect purchasing action. Unless there is a click to a landing page, it's a Glance and Forget channel.

- **Email.** The best use for email is when you have built your own list of raving fans. Email results are lousy when sent to people who haven't opted in to your message. So if you're writing to your opt-in list of customers (or inquiries), write content to provoke curiosity that leads them to click to a landing page, leading to the possibility of Short-Term Comprehension. When the email was only opened, but there wasn't a click, then it is a Glance and Forget channel.

- **Websites/Landing Pages.** If someone searched and happened upon your website, and if the bounce rate is high, you have a Glance and Forget website. If, on the other hand, you have a landing page with valuable content and call-to-action, or CTA (for example, opting in to an email list), you have a shot at Short-Term Comprehension, and in some instances, Long-Term Memory Comprehension.

- **Short Video.** A short video will likely be a Glance and Forget channel unless you have a call-to-action leading to a landing page with a CTA or opt-in to your list. When that occurs, you might be able to lead to Short-Term Comprehension.

- **Long Video (or a Video Sales Letter).** When viewed all the way to the end, a long video should result in Short-Term Comprehension, and possibly Long-Term Memory Comprehension and a sale, when there is an effective CTA.

- **Direct Mail Postcard.** There's not much space on a postcard, and with so much postcard competition in the mailbox, most postcards are a Glance and Forget channel. A thoughtfully created postcard can result in Short-Term Comprehension, however. And if you have a strong CTA, you can move a postcard message to Long-Term Memory

Comprehension if the person acts by either calling for information or making a purchase.

- **Direct Mail Package.** The ability to deliver long persuasive copy is the value of direct mail. Let's not kid ourselves: most direct mail is never opened and goes directly into the trash, making it a Glance and Forget channel to most recipients. But when the recipient is curious upon seeing the outer envelope, opens it, and dives into a long-form letter, brochure, or reads an insert or order device with your offer, you've achieved at least Short-Term Comprehension. When the creative and copywriting effectively persuades and sells, you lead your prospect to Long-Term Memory Comprehension. When you do that, you can score the sale.

o2o CHANNEL LEAPING

The most strategically planned marketing effort can be sabotaged when you are moving your prospective customer or donor from an offline channel to an online channel for transactions. An instance where you are selling offline, but accepting the response online, is an offline to online (o2o) channel leap. Redirection must be carefully designed, tested, and refined to maximize the conversion process.

There is often a disconnect between concept and execution of taking a prospect from offline to online. You may be so close to the process that you sometimes assume a seamless o2o flow, but while fumbling around a keyboard, the prospect's attention can be diverted. The online order experience can be clunky or even confusing. Sometimes too much is asked on the online order screen, and information overload sets in. Or we assume the customer is tech-savvy when in fact, they're not. Orders and carts are abandoned because the prospect gives up.

What to do to ensure a seamless o2o leap? Here are five recommendations:

1. **Clarity Rules.** Create a detailed flow chart of every possible path a prospect could take before they press "buy" to see if there is any unanswered or confusing language or visuals. Ensure that there are no dead-ends, and allow them to back up. And, be sure the form they're

returning to is still populated with their original entries, rather than being shown an infuriating screen full of blank fields.

2. **Roadmap the Journey.** Manage expectations for your prospect with an overview of the process, why it'll be worth their time, and how easy and quick it will be, especially if placing an order has multiple options.

3. **Wireframe to Visualize.** If you, the marketer, are having trouble visualizing how it all works, just imagine how confused your customer will be. Developing even a crude wireframe will help ensure you don't overlook something, or that the process unfolds logically and obviously.

4. **Clear Copy.** Write to the reading level of your audience, but remember that online channels tend to be one where people are more rushed and scanning. They don't always read for detail. Make it clear and simple.

5. **Tell and Sell with Video.** People may not read copy as closely online, but they are apt to invest time watching a video with tips on how to place their order. It can save the customer time, and help reduce abandoned carts.

The back-end programming of online order systems are usually outside the responsibility of the marketing team. But, if you're the marketer or copywriter, you need to put serious thought and effort into the customer-facing side, so it's clear, friendly, and quick. Your prospect forms a lasting impression of your entire organization when you have an o2o channel leap requirement. And, if it's muddled or worse, you may never have another opportunity to make it positive.

CHAPTER 12

COMING FULL CIRCLE: PATHWAYS AS STRATEGY

Strategy is often the first item discussed in a marketing plan. Unfortunately, strategy may be among the most misunderstood tools a marketer can use. I'll admit that over the years I've struggled with defining strategy. Too often, strategy quickly morphs into tactics.

A NEW TEMPLATE FOR STRATEGY

With my research and identification of the seven pathways in the mind, I believe that combined they create a new and better template for devising strategy. Not only does this template force you to think more broadly, conceptually, and deeply, a strategy statement using these seven pathways takes you full circle.

The following example is from a strategy statement I wrote for a retailer. It uses the seven pathways, and can be an example of how you create your own strategy statement.

Persona: Our strategy is let the [organization name] customer self-select her personality ...

Stimulate: and inspire her to find her style and share it.

Calm: Her discovery will be emotionally affirmed by her social network of friends ...

Position: ... and reinforce that she has made a fashionable style choice.

Storytelling: The inspiring story of the fashion designer ...

Interpret: ... delights her with the affordably of an exclusive offer.

Permission: She concludes "this is good, this is smart, I feel good about myself and I give myself permission to buy" from her trusted style resource, [organization name].

Download this new template for strategy statement at CustomerMindCode. com/Resources.

THE BIG PICTURE OF EACH PERSONA

By now, you should have in your mind an idea of which of the 12 personas are the dominant persona of your prospects and customers. Perhaps you recognize a couple of the personas and how you can combine them. Or maybe you imagine still a different persona inspired by what has been written here.

In some cases, any one of the 12 personas could be close to your situation, but with changing a few sentences or bullet points, you may be able to more closely zero in on your prospective customer or donor.

In the previous chapters, you have been given a taste of each persona and what that individual would think in each phase of the pathways. In the interest of making it easier for you to absorb the complete persona, in the following chapters the personas that were shared earlier are repeated. Here, you can read the complete pathway process for each persona for easier reference.

CHAPTER 13

PERSONA #1: TRAILBLAZERS/ EARLY ADOPTERS

1. CORE PERSONA VALUES

Deep down, I yearn to be the first to acquire what's new. I'm an "innovator." I thrive on blazing a new trail with what's new and cutting edge. I will stand in line for hours to be the first to acquire the latest, greatest, and newest product as it is being introduced. Ahead of the curve? That's me! It makes me feel important. Some call me a geek.

I have the money and financial means to be ahead of the pack. Yeah, I know the prices are often higher to be the first to have it. But it's worth it to me. I want to be the first to have everything, so that I can flash it around.

I'm passionate and deeply desire to be among the few in the know so I can acquire it first. And when I find something new and cool that I really like, you can bet I'm going to advocate the product and become an evangelist for the product creator. But companies should beware: if the product sucks, I'll tell the world. I'm always online, chatting, posting, and making my opinion known. My friends and I stick together to alert everyone of product fails.

2. STIMULATE EMOTION

I fear being left behind and missing out on the latest and newest. My emotional fears are stoked when I'm not the first to know. I read, watch videos and am up-to-date in what's new. I also research information to check out if something is real or a hoax. This is a mental competition to me. I must stay current because I don't want to ever feel behind-the-curve and slip on the Diffusion of Innovations curve from being an "Innovator" to an "Early Adopter." I would just die if I slipped even farther to the boring and unimaginative "Early Majority." My peers would recognize my downfall, and that could be the end of my status as a leading-edge "Innovator."

3. CALM THE MIND

When I experience calm, it's because I'm surrounded by the latest and greatest. I feel like a kid in a candy store. I'm confident when I have access to new products before they are ever made available to the world. I'm a sucker for getting the inside scoop, especially when the inside skinny is for me and only a few select people.

I'm smart and savvy. When companies deliver information and feed my ego, I reward them with loyalty and social following.

When my mind is calmed, I'm open to engagement. Convince me, and I'll be a loyal follower and evangelist.

4. POSITION / REPOSITION

If you want my attention, products must be positioned as being new, innovative, and leading-edge. And you must make good on that positioning. I'll turn a product away if it looks like yesterday's news or breakthrough. There's a lot of competition out there, and if you want my loyalty, don't let a competitor beat you to the punch with a newer and sexier positioning statement. So you'd better be researching your competition and compare your product, because if you don't, I will.

I have a short attention span, so product positioning needs to be freshened often to stay ahead of the curve. I expect the companies I rely upon to have regular brainstorming and planning to review the existing product position, figure out what's out-of-date, and strategize about how the next bright, shiny object is going to be created.

5. TELL A STORY

I think I'm pretty cool, especially with technology. But you know, I like to hear a good story, too. As long as there is a point, you can engage me and I'll even stick with you. But don't waste my time.

Tell me a story about how I can be envied by my friends. Or tell me how I can anticipate being the first to get a product with the anticipation and joy of having it.

But I want the story to feel like I'm the star. I want to walk right into the story line. I'll probably empathize with the hero of the story, and I'm going to remember a good story for a while (and might just tell it over and over to my friends).

6. INTERPRET

I'm usually a few steps ahead of most people, so I've got things figured out before the marketer does. Tell me if you think you must, but I can figure out the benefits. I like features and bright shiny objects. You see, I expect there will be no issues with a product. I expect superiority and quality. So you'd better have credible arguments in place that takes me to that logical place in my mind.

Listen, I'm not all that concerned about price. I'll pay what I think its worth, and I'll pay a premium if the situation is right. Still, I like to feel like I got a good deal, even if the seller threw in a little "gimme" with enough value that I can brag about getting something for nothing.

I do want to see a guarantee, but spare me the nonsense and just tell me that you stand behind your product.

7. PERMISSION TO ACT

Here's what motivates me to act: Knowing a product is for real, it's new and advanced, and that I'm going to be the first to have it!

If I can recall a past experience that gave me great pleasure, and proved to myself once again that I'm an innovator, I'll give myself permission to act. I use my gut instinct to make a decision, but when I know it's right, I'll freely give myself permission to buy it now.

CHAPTER 14

PERSONA #2:
MY BRAND/MY LIFESTYLE/
MY GROWTH

1. CORE PERSONA VALUES

My personal brand demands attention. My look, lifestyle, and personal growth they are all at the core of my being. The fact is when I receive a compliment of any kind, my head swells with pride. I love to be glitzy glamorous, and when I'm flattered, it reinforces that I am eternally young. You might call me a fashionista. If looking good above all else means being physically uncomfortable, then that's the way it is.

I'm comfortable spending money, so I can brag about the experience. My lifestyle choices and brand are made to position myself as the envy of people around me. I want to imagine myself as a jet setter who travels extensively and who dresses the part.

It's also important to me that I grow my mind and my skills because knowledge is highly valued and is a part of my personal brand. Possessing an intellectual acumen for leadership positions me as someone who is important.

2. STIMULATE EMOTION

I am highly protective of my brand. I constantly fear my brand and my status will be lost. As a result, I am constantly grooming myself, both literally and figuratively, so that I have an edge in my career and personal life. Maintaining that level of personal brand requires ongoing attention and I'm always on guard about protecting my brand. I fear my lifestyle will come under threat. I fear that I won't be seen at the right place or that I'm not growing intellectually.

- I fear being left behind and that my personal brand will suffer.
- I fear that I will not stand apart from the crowd and that I will blend in and be merely average.
- My appearance is a personal brand in a trademark.
- My appearance must support my lifestyle.
- I wouldn't be caught underdressed or not looking right when in public.
- I'm not afraid to stand apart from the crowd.
- If my appearance isn't just right, I fear suffering the consequences to my personal brand.
- I fear my lifestyle could vanish.
- I fear I won't keep up with personal growth opportunities so I am on constant alert.

Some days I'm a fashionista. Professionally I may be a sales representative. I am highly engaged in personal development and go to seminars, read, and enjoy networking.

3. CALM THE MIND

I am at my calmest when I know that my brand, lifestyle, and growth are being supported. You can calm my mind by feeding my ego and telling me that I have a good appearance, or you can feed my ego with positivity. I like things that are aesthetically pleasing. I like to feel I will learn something just by reading your sales message. I want to know that I can achieve more. When there is the promise that I will learn something or be inspired in any message, I am engaged.

- Praise and compliments will reinforce that I am fulfilling my personal brand strategy. I want to be assured that my personal brand will be advanced whenever I am seen with a product.
- I yearn for words of affirmation. Design must be up-to-date and evolve with the times.

- My head will swell with pride and I'll feel like a million dollars when I receive praise from people around me, whether it's because of my appearance or my knowledge.

I am quickly and easily calmed. But if you don't calm my sensitive personality and emotion early on in our conversation, you will lose me.

4. POSITION / REPOSITION

I like to see that an organization has my best interest at heart. I'm concerned about styles and priorities changing with every season. It's vital to me that any company I do business with is current and with the times. I look for an organization as a resource to enhance my personal brand and my perceived trademark.

My friends and my relationships are important to me. I tend to band together with people who think like me. We are highly interactive and we can be snarky about those who appear to be yesterday's news. I want to stand apart from the crowd. I seek out products and services that will deliver uniqueness. I don't want to be a copycat. I don't want to see a company claiming something to be their own, but learning it was ripped it off from someplace else. When I find a company that is unique and serves my needs, I'll end up doing the selling for them!

5. TELL A STORY

I have a great imagination. I like to hear stories from companies I do business with. They can set themselves apart by being unique. That is deeply desirable to me.

Because I am brand and style conscious, the story can include a role model. I like to hear about people who have come from struggle and who have succeeded with changes in their lives. I like to know an organization has had that same "come from behind" experience. This helps enable me to know that my own doubts can be overcome. As someone interested in personal growth, sometimes I doubt my own ability to achieve goals. I want to see that people just like me can achieve the same goals that I have. I like to know that someone has turned around their life because of certain decisions and actions that they have taken. This makes the story credible.

I like to hear stories about how someone's life was changed because their look caught the eye of a lover, employer, or someone who could make them famous. I'm drawn to photographs, illustrations, and elegant design.

6. INTERPRET

Even though I have been given a good positioning and storyline about a product, I like to have it interpreted so I can see how it can impact me. I want to know that the outward aesthetics will cultivate an attitude for me that will make me feel better about myself.

I also want a guarantee that is less about numbers and more about feeling. This is all about what a product or service will do for me. Price is a consideration, but I'm less concerned about price as long as I see a benefit in purchasing a product. Value is most important to me even if the price point is hefty. I will make it work for me if I see the value of it, but you will have to show me how the price point makes sense and delivers on what will make me feel better about myself.

7. PERMISSION TO ACT

I have to admit that my purchase decisions are usually based on the emotion that I feel at the time. It's a part of my instinct. It's a part of my decision of whether it will advance my brand, lifestyle or personal growth. I need to visually see and instinctively feel when an offer is right for me. I need to be able to step into the offer and see how it will fit with me for my lifestyle choices. When that happens, I will feel a chill that instinctively tells me that I can now give myself permission to purchase.

Past memories are very strong for me. I remember when I was given compliments in the past, and they made me feel great. That's the power of a new look and a new brand. That's the emotion I must feel to give myself permission to act.

CHAPTER 15

PERSONA #3:
MONEY MATTERS

1. CORE PERSONA VALUES

I'm a practical and sensible person. I have common sense. My decisions are usually based on a combination of price and value. I don't always look for the lowest price in every situation, but I do look for the greatest value, and I'm careful with my money. I'm frugal. I work hard. I don't believe in needlessly spending my money. I don't need thrills or frills. Most important to me is accumulating money, not possessions.

I wish the world were more sensible. I know I can't change the world, but I think I can be of influence to people around me. How I spend money becomes a badge that I wear on my sleeve. Don't misunderstand me; I'm not seeking notoriety. I really don't even seek attention. Rather, I quietly lead my life with a certain smugness that will ultimately enable me to live comfortably. I don't want the financial pressures that so many people feel. For me, money matters a lot. I will seek out the greatest value I can find, and I will be quietly proud of my accomplishment.

2. STIMULATE EMOTION

I fear waste. I fear being sucked into situations that threatens my pragmatism. I don't want to be walked down a primrose path that leads to wasted time and money. And I certainly don't want to be seen as unnecessarily extravagant.

As I review marketing materials, I fear that a product may not support who I am or my values. I fear overpaying. I especially fear I have overpaid on something I have recently purchased. Seeing a sale after I have made a purchase puts me off. I don't want stability in my life to be rocked.

- I'm naturally skeptical of all claims.
- I fear being misled and ripped off and being betrayed by anyone or any organization that I do business with.
- I fear my hard-earned money will be wasted.
- I fear I will be taken advantage of.

Because of my fears, I am less apt to make quick decisions. I can quickly have buyer's remorse about any buying decision that I make. When I am reminded of my fears, I seek information that will help reassure me and calm my mind.

3. CALM THE MIND

Calm my mind with the promise there will be value and a marketer's message won't be a waste of my time. But the message must be genuine, without overdoing it. I'm naturally more skeptical than most. Too much flare and you can quickly turn me off. I will see through any over-hype of a marketing message. It must be sincere. Sincerity and steadiness will calm my mind.

- I must be assured I'm getting value
- I need access to data, so I can conduct my own research
- Give me an initial illustration how the product is a good value with charts, graphs, or numbers
- Testimonials, early on, from people like me adds affirmation
- Make me feel more secure than I will with competitors

I'm naturally apprehensive and hesitate about parting with my hard-earned money. I consider myself stable and I don't want that aspect of my life disrupted. I must be assured that a marketer isn't wasting my time. When a marketer demonstrates how they have my best interests at heart, I'll reward them with my business.

4. POSITION / REPOSITION

A product positioned with value is essential for me. I want to see that I am smart when I buy from an organization. When I see that an investment will pay off over time that can be a strong positioning to me. I must see fundamental intrinsic value that will appeal to my very core. My pragmatism is very deeply ingrained, so anything I see shouldn't be extravagant or particularly flashy. I like down-to-earth. For example, when I contribute to a specific type of cause, I want to see it demonstrated that most of my financial gift will flow to the people or the situation where money is intended to go.

I like to accumulate financially smart assets. Things are not very important to me. I like to research information. It's very helpful when a marketer positions themselves as the resource of the best information. A marketer sharing research for me is helpful. But that information must be credible. I will seek independent validation of anything that is claimed by a marketer's positioning. I'm adept at numbers so I will look for facts and costs in a matter-of-fact, pragmatic kind of way. That's how I will most likely accept a marketer's message.

5. TELL A STORY

A sensible story resonates for me. The tone of the story needs to feature someone like me who is unassuming, who doesn't flaunt possessions, and quietly lives their lives knowing that they make smart choices. I'm fine with hearing about someone who is wealthy as long as they are not flashy. Their story can be a template for my story. I like to hear things like that.

I want to see that nothing is wasted. I want the story to substantiate claims credibly. The story is even enhanced if I can see how someone was not taken advantage of.

I can be a numbers geek, so I like data woven into a story. Include charts, graphs, and numbers, and you can keep me engaged for a long time. When I'm thinking like an investor, for example, I'm drawn to a story that illustrates how insider information or hidden information was used to make significant money. Metaphors help, too. This helps me connect the dots between myself and what a company is offering.

Most important in the story is that I must see a value message. The cost is less important to me than the value it returns. Sure, I'm interested in a deal. But that doesn't necessarily mean cheap.

6. INTERPRET

Interpretation of product features and benefits are very important to me. I need a considerable amount of logic in the sales message to take me to a place where I will consider responding. I like details. But I also need those details translated into benefits. Those can be the tipping points for me.

Prices need to be explained to me in a way that shows value. I like to see pricing broken down into ways such as price per day, price per unit, or the long-term value of a product after time. I've got to be sold.

A strong guarantee is essential for me. A guarantee that is specific and is stated in long-term value, such as 90 days versus 30 days, means a lot. When you present me with a 30-day guarantee, my mental clock starts ticking so that as I approached the 30th day, it creates uncertainty for me and I wonder if I should return the product. More time is better.

7. PERMISSION TO ACT

I sense chills when I see a great value for my money. This is what it takes to go to an emotional place where I feel I can give myself permission to act.

Because I am so pragmatic, I enjoy accumulation of possessions only when it makes sense in my life.

Past memories are strong motivators for me. When I am taken back to something that gave me great joy that I still enjoy today, and was a great value, I'm reminded that it was a smart decision at the time. I like to logically and emotionally conclude that a decision is right for me. I must be taken to a place where I say to myself, "This is smart, this is good, and I give myself permission to act."

CHAPTER 16

PERSONA #4:
ON FINANCIAL EDGE

1. CORE PERSONA VALUES

I always feel strapped. My credit isn't very good. I often don't fit in to traditional financial services and banking. Unfortunately I'm not always able to pay my bills on time.

It's a struggle. I'm not proud of my situation, but I do the best I can to manage my finances. Sometimes I just overspend. I'm not good at math. I guess my reading skills aren't so good either. I don't tend to pay a lot of attention to accountability. I go about my life not realizing that I have exhausted all of the money available to me. Other times it's just that I don't make enough money to pay all the bills. As the saying goes, "there's too much month left at the end of the money."

I'll admit I don't know how to manage money. It wasn't taught to me. Or maybe I just wasn't paying attention in school.

I'm doing my best, but I sometimes fall short of what the world expects of me. I live paycheck to paycheck. I'm afraid of people taking advantage of me, yet I'm often open to helping others just like me. I'm part of my silent community. That's my life and I struggle to make changes and improvements to my standard of living.

2. STIMULATE EMOTION

I fear that someday I'm not going to have the money to pay for basic items like food. I can't afford good nutritious food, so I get what's available and fast.

Earning enough money is an ongoing struggle and money problems are constantly on my mind. Sometimes I use a bank as a place to keep my money. But a lot of times I simply look for alternative ways to keep my money. I like credit cards. Sometimes I have to get a short-term payday loan. My emotion is stimulated when I see a place that will give me a credit lifeline. But all too often I'm unable to charge any more on a credit card—that's if I even have one that I can use. So I have to look for alternatives.

Because of the difficulty for me to understand how to manage money, I sometimes feel threatened and intimidated by all of the fine print of credit offers.

Living day-to-day, sometimes I wake up in the morning not knowing how I'm going to get through the week. The next pay day can't come fast enough. Sometimes I wonder if I'm going to have a place to live. I'm especially concerned about losing my car. Without a car, I can't get to work. If I have to choose what to pay first, I'll pay for my car over other things. I can always sleep in my car for a few nights if needed. A lot of people around me don't know what I'm dealing with deep inside.

3. CALM THE MIND

I am most calm when I can see a pathway ahead of me where I won't be short on cash. When I know I can find a place to live that will accept my situation and late rent payment, I'm temporarily calmed. I would be calmed if I knew that my car was not going to a pose a problem for me. Knowing I can provide for my family also calms me.

I hope to be able to work with people and companies who can empathize and appreciate my situation. Being able to trust someone and an organization would be helpful in my life. When I see someone like me who needs a hand, I do what I can to help them. Especially family. I know that someday I'm going to need help, too.

Life is a struggle. And I do my best to put on a positive face. But if I can just see a chance to get ahead, I will feel much better about myself. I just need a break.

4. POSITION / REPOSITION

I'm most comfortable working with people and an organization that understands my problem and won't take advantage of my situation. I want to feel that they have my best interests at heart. A company that approaches me in a trusting way, that offers a helping hand, and is not judgmental means a lot to me.

I want to be talked to in plain language, but don't talk down to me! My reading skills aren't the best, so I need to be able to understand any terms or conditions. Hearing a message sometimes is the best for me. I like to talk to people in person or at least hear a recorded message or watch a video.

I don't want to feel like I am being investigated if I need money or credit. I want my life to be private, and an organization who can reassure me of my privacy is important.

5. TELL A STORY

There are so many people just like me. I like to hear how an organization has helped someone in a situation like mine. The story should tell me how easy it is to do business with a company who understands that I need non-traditional approaches. It's important to me that an organization empathizes with my situation. When I see a testimonial from someone else, it helps to reassure me and I'm more apt to give this organization a chance. Stories are important to me. Sometimes I feel so alone, and with so few lifelines, that hearing how others were helped will make me feel better.

6. INTERPRET

While it's important for me to understand all of the details, I admit that I don't always pay a lot of attention to them. Sometimes I barely understand them. I just want a solution for what's most important to me right now. It's hard for me to think very far into the future. I want to know how a product or organization can help me at this moment, not next month.

Since I'm not very good with details, I just need to have the one, two, or three most important things that I can understand spelled out for me. Don't make this complicated, if you do, I'll have to pass on it because if I can't understand it then I can't act on it.

7. PERMISSION TO ACT

I give myself permission to act if I can see that this is a product that's going to help me right now. I need to know that it's accessible to me. I need to know that I'm not going to be burned or otherwise regret my decision. I'll even take a chance sometimes if I'm uncertain.

Some days are desperate for me. Make it easy, understandable, and accessible right now. I don't want any hassle. If it seems like it's in my best interest, I will quickly make a decision to act.

CHAPTER 17

PERSONA #5:
RIGHT THING TO DO

1. CORE PERSONA VALUES

I'm a person who takes the high road. I make decisions based on what are right for me, my family, my health, the environment, and more. My persona is one who judges and makes decisions that are based on if a product or cause supports my belief system of doing the right thing. Sometimes I will fall on a sword for any cause. Some say I'm an activist.

I believe every decision should be based on if it's the right choice to support whatever deep-seated values I possess. A decision must support my belief system, or I will have misgivings and buyer's remorse. I feel affirmed when decisions give me permission to feel good about myself, the people around me, the earth, and our culture.

I recycle. I try to choose food that is nutritious or organic, and grown with as little negative impact on the earth as possible. I drive a fuel-efficient vehicle. In the back of my mind, I must know that my purchase decisions won't have a negative impact on culture or the world around me. I want to see, from marketers, how their product is the right choice for me. Cost isn't always an issue.

The world and our culture will spiral downward unless we all participate in turning things around. I don't want to have any regrets. I will do my part. I wish other people would share my sentiments. I'm fearful we will leave the world in a worse place than it was given to us. My righteous-based decisions are my small way of making myself and the world a better place. I sleep better at night when I have taken the high road.

2. STIMULATE EMOTION

I fear my moral compass will be compromised. I am shaken when things go wrong. It is unnerving to me when I see others being taken advantage of, and when our culture and society take directional turns away from what our belief systems and foundational principles should be. I'm a bit negative about the world around me, and to a degree I look down on others who don't live up to certain standards.

My fears include:

- If the right things aren't supported, the world and our culture will spiral downward.
- People around me aren't doing their part.
- The world is ending up a worse state than how it was given to me.
- Fear of regretting that I didn't do more to make the world a better place.

I believe that issues such as climate change are huge, and needs to be addressed now, at any cost. I want to choose automobiles that are the most environmentally friendly. It's the right thing to do!

3. CALM THE MIND

I am at peace with people and organizations who share the same journey, path and values that I do. I simply cannot accept mediocrity. I want to see exacting standards. This is how my emotion is calmed. I want to see that an organization is going the extra mile and that their commitment is to leave the world a better place.

Here are other ways that my mind is calmed:

- When a decision supports my deep values, the price doesn't matter.
- I feel good about myself and my beliefs when a product supports my point of view.

- I want to be assured that the world will be a better place because of an organization's commitment, and that they are on my side.
- I want to see how my decisions will help support a more sustainable world.

I am loyal to any organization once I can trust it. I need to be shown how that organization will make the world a better place. I want them to reciprocate with their loyalty and commitment to my belief system. I will reward them with my business. When it's demonstrated to me that an organization has started a movement to bring more people to my way of thinking, that's an added bonus and oftentimes a decision tipping point.

4. POSITION / REPOSITION

It's important to me that I see a company's core values prominently displayed. I want to know that this organization is credible and trustable. I seek high standards. I don't expect any more from an organization than I would personally deliver or stand by if the roles were reversed. I will be loyal to a company who is positioned within the scope of my values. I want the internal satisfaction that the decisions I make are aligned with that of anyone I do business with. I have strong work ethics and character. I want a better tomorrow, so it's essential that a product is positioned for making the world a better place.

5. TELL A STORY

I enjoy reading stories about people who have a deep desire to do the right thing. These people are my heroes. There are people who would save a life. I want to be just like those people because in my heart I believe that every good deed is rewarded.

When I can identify with a hero, no matter what the product, I am engaged in the message. I need to know this story exists so that there are no regrets in making a purchase. I want to know that someone felt better about himself or herself and could sleep better at night. I want to know that my pride and my moral compass are strong. I want to see how mediocrity can be overcome. I believe that ethics and character will always prevail. When the story is strong, the cost of the product doesn't matter to me.

I'm especially drawn to stories where someone has created a movement, or a persuasive way to advance a position. Big ideas enthrall me. When I see myself in the story and see my role as part of something larger, I will buy quickly and participate almost without question.

6. INTERPRET

Because I believe in doing the right thing, information needs to be interpreted for me so that I can clearly see that an organization supports my beliefs. There can be no issues with any product or service. Any logic in the interpretation of a product's offer must serve an important purpose so that I can see it supports my point of view.

I take a logical approach to my thinking, so a logical argument that can be built for me enables me to trust in the interpretation. A guarantee needs to go beyond price and time value. It needs to go to the heart of my attitude where I feel gratified that I have made the right choice. I don't tend to get over consumed with cost. I recognize the extra price is sometimes what it takes to support my belief system and values.

7. PERMISSION TO ACT

I sense a feeling of peace when I make a decision to act because I see it supports my belief system. I simply cannot have any apprehension that my decision is anything less than the right thing to do. Sometimes a tipping point for me is within an offer such as a bonus or doing something good for a cause I support.

When I recall a past positive experience that supports and reinforces my belief, my mind opens. I get chills and feel a physiological reaction whenever I do something that supports my belief system. By releasing myself from skepticism I give myself permission to act.

CHAPTER 18

PERSONA #6: LOVE AND SOCIAL RELATIONSHIPS

1. CORE PERSONA VALUES

My life revolves around relationships. I am affirmed by love and acceptance from loved ones, family and friends. I'll admit that sometimes I'm insecure about myself. I highly value being loved, wanted and desired. I need to have a partner in my life to feel fulfilled. When that happens, all is well in the world. Without a life partner, there is emptiness that I crave to have filled. I turn to family and friends to fill that void. The center of my life is to be liked, and I seek affirmations for everything I do.

My purchase decisions are influenced by what my friends will think about me. I am naturally attracted to anything that could make me more lovable and likable to others. I love being active on social media. I am careful about the photos I post because I want them to be a statement about me. Selfies with influential people are important to me, and I will regularly post about those experiences. It affirms who I am and it elevates my self-worth.

2. STIMULATE EMOTION

With my basic need to have people close to me, my fear is that a purchase decision will make people look down on me. I have a strong fear that anything can jeopardize a relationship. I need affirmation from friends. I fear missing out.

Some days I find myself living on social media as I clamor for attention and affirmation. My fears include:

- I won't be loved.
- A relationship could falter.
- Being disliked, discredited, or rejected.
- That my "street cred" will be diminished and social ranking negatively impacted.

I fear being left out of social plans made by other people. I don't need to be the center of attention. I'm perfectly happy to be on the sidelines. It would hurt me tremendously if I were not included with friends and if I were banished from any social activities.

3. CALM THE MIND

When all is well in my life I am calm. When things are out of balance in my life and are not going well I will be distracted and stressed. So I need to be calmed through empathy. To me it's less about the promise of what your product or service will ultimately do for me, but how a company opens up to me and listens to me. I need to have time invested in me from an organization to calm my mind. But once I feel that I am being listened to I am more receptive to a message. These are a few ways that I can be calmed:

- I need to feel that my friends and family will agree with me because I have followed an organization or I purchase a specific product.
- I like to feel security, knowing that I can expand relationships and my circle of influence.
- I want to feel there is better harmony in my life so that I feel a sense of acceptance from others.
- I am calmed when my "street cred" and social ranking is boosted

I'll admit I am prone to mood swings, so when my mood is moderated and I am calm, I am more open.

4. POSITION / REPOSITION

A marketer's positioning needs to support my deep internal need for building relationships. Make a promise and demonstrate that by engaging with a marketer's product or service that my life will be more fulfilled.

I'm sensitive to my credibility so a marketer must constantly illustrate in its positioning how it supports me. I warm up to positioning that:

- Enhances love and the experience with my partner.
- Strengthens relationships.
- Elevates my "street cred."

5. TELL A STORY

My emotion is aroused when I hear a story about romance with a dose of eroticism. This brings me more deeply into the message because it affirms my feeling about love. Sometimes I go into a trance, and I deeply desire to be part of a story like that. My life sometimes has emptiness and I want to know that there are other people who share my feelings. I want to know that other people experience moments like these in their lives. But I want to see goodness for other people so that I can see the light of day shining on myself.

A story can help to alleviate my insecurities. I like to share stories on social media. I like to be the first to get the news out fast so I look like I am a trend setter, and not a follower. This elevates my mood. I consider it a selfie moment.

6. INTERPRET

I like to understand how making a decision will positively influence my life. I don't need a lot of logical explanation, but I do need some. I need to understand benefits, pricing, and a guarantee. I'd love to read about a guarantee that says I will never have rejection again in my life. Not realistic, but that's what I would like to see.

I don't want to say that price is no object, but if I can clearly see how a product will work for me and the price and the benefits make sense, I will make an emotional decision to move forward.

Both features and benefits are essential for me to understand. Benefits need to illustrate how I am going to feel whole in my relationships.

7. PERMISSION TO ACT

As a naturally emotional person, I like to recall fond memories of the past. Whenever those times occur, I feel emptiness. I want to feel like I am going to be fulfilled. Past memory recall is a strong motivator for me, but I have both negative and positive recollections. If I feel negative, I may not be moved to take action. But if I feel positive, especially if I feel a revelation of what something will do to strengthen love and social relationships, I will be inclined to give myself permission to act.

Let me feel chills and I will be pushed over the edge. This is where I conclude that a decision is right for me.

CHAPTER 19

PERSONA #7:
ADRENALINE SEEKERS:
OPPORTUNISTS

1. CORE PERSONA VALUES

I am convinced that I can beat the system. Whenever there is an opportunity or chance that I will prevail "over the man," I experience a physical adrenaline rush. Money isn't the big motivator. Feeling that I can beat the system or beat the house—whether it's the stock market or a casino—gives me a rush like none other.

I can smell opportunity, and I play to win. Money is a scorecard. I don't always need to win a big pile of cash; I just need to score. A small win is still a win, and it's worthy of bragging rights. I'm a realist, but I'm also a dreamer. I like to be given the opportunity to see myself as part of the story and dream big because when that happens, my adrenaline motivates me to play along.

I'm a risk taker and I crave winning. Losing isn't taken easily, but it happens. However, you're not going to hear about any of my losses. My losses are quickly erased from my memory grooves and they're replaced with the memory of past wins. Adrenaline gushes when I'm introduced to an opportunity that I sense is an alternative to traditional approaches.

2. STIMULATE EMOTION

I fear missing big opportunities. I fear being left out of the action when I can seize an opportunity. It's often fueled by the opportunity to make or to win money. I fear the establishment, and for that reason, I like to seek out my own path.

Here's what I believe:

- I think the odds are stacked against me.
- I fear for missed opportunities that may never come back again, so I seize them.
- No one has my back, so I believe I have to make a mark on the world on my own.

I want to believe I can beat the house or beat the system. The psychological lift of winning trumps the dollars. I don't like to follow the establishment. I seek hidden opportunities to make money.

3. CALM THE MIND

I'm satisfied when I am calm. If I can see a "told you so" moment, I want to be rewarded with how I can participate. It's even more satisfying when I see how I can beat the system. It's especially important for me to feel that I'm in an exclusive group, an insider, and get in on the early action. I need to know up front that I'm going to learn something of value by consuming a marketer's message. When I feel I can learn something and benefit from a message without buying anything, I'm in. Of course what often happens is that I read an entire message, consume it, and find out I need just a little more information that can only be had by purchasing. I get it. If I want to have the full solution, it means I have to take the bait.

Here's what else I feel:

- An adrenaline rush is both stimulating and calming to me at the same time.
- When I decide to go for it, my mind goes into a trancelike state.
- I'm highly motivated when I live on the edge
- As someone who lives for the adrenalin rush, disappointment can be intense, and I never want to experience that feeling.

My mind may never be totally calm, but if I feel satisfied that I'm going to get something out of it, I'll continue absorbing the marketing message.

4. POSITION / REPOSITION

I want to see a path toward winning, so I want to see opportunities positioned for me that are exclusive and offered on a limited time basis. I'm selfish, and I don't want to share in the joy of victory; I want to be able to boast about it. Turn me into a winner and deliver on it, and a company will have me as a customer for life.

But I'm not easily snookered into things. I need to see that there is a track record where others have been successful. I like to read testimonials and have other winners shown. When that happens, the message is more credible to me. I seek authority, especially if I'm investing my money. But I also admit to being a high roller wannabe when the bright lights sparkle.

I want to see action and possibility. When I do, I will give an organization the time of day. But if I don't get quick results or have a quick win, I'll move on. I want to know that an organization will help me feed my passion.

5. TELL A STORY

I want to hear a private story; one that I feel is just for me, and no one else. A story heightens my senses. A story tells me how someone made it big, with the inside secrets of getting there.

I crave having a plan that is unconventional. I believe I can go into it alone and not follow mainstream thought. So a marketer's story needs to bring to life either someone or something that shows me how it's done without the establishment. I view money as a scorecard, so a marketer's story is of most interest when it revolves around money.

I really get into a story where someone like me, who has the odds stacked against them, takes a risk and wins. And if it's a once-in-a-lifetime opportunity, my adrenaline soars because I fear that if I don't taken action, I'll miss out.

6. INTERPRET

Even though my adrenaline makes me highly emotional, I still like to have a logical argument. I'm a bit torn between logic and emotion. The adrenaline junkie side of me wants to instinctively act without significant heaps of logic. Yet I can be taken down a path through a story that builds to a logical argument and draws me in. It helps me rationalize my decision-making.

I want to be guaranteed that I have the opportunity reserved for myself. For me, money is useful to bringing me enjoyment. If I think I can beat the system, I don't object to paying a price. But the price needs to be logically spelled out for me.

7. PERMISSION TO ACT

I feel chills when I'm emotionally taken to a place where my adrenaline takes over. When that happens, I simply give myself permission to impulsively act. But I want to feel that an organization has my best interest in mind. That's where I say to myself, "This is good, this is smart, and I give myself the permission required to respond."

When I see a pattern of my past behavior that I've benefited from, I'm especially drawn to act. I will instinctively feel when it's the right decision for me, and when I do, I'll make a quick decision. Chills are important to me. That's when I know my adrenaline is pumping, and it's what drives me to make decisions.

CHAPTER 20

PERSONA #8: SAFE PLAYERS

1. CORE PERSONA VALUES

I play my life safely. I don't like to take risks. For that reason, I'm often sought after by my risk-taking friends because I am a problem solver. I think of myself as unassuming in my approach to buying decisions. Financial risks are out of the question. All my earthly possessions are important to me, and I protect and nurture them. I am fearful of making a decision that will result in loss, and losses aren't limited to only money. As a professional, my belief in safety extends into my relationships with clients. I'll admit that I am more pessimistic than optimistic about outcomes. I tend to doubt some choices that I make, so I approach things very carefully.

I am inclined to create a firewall around myself so that I don't have to deal with problems. I think of myself as a problem solver. I am loyal to organizations that help keep me safe.

2. STIMULATE EMOTION

I fear risk. I abhor it. I fear risking everything imaginable: losing money, failing health, breaking relationships, and much more. I'm often on edge, so it's easy to stimulate my emotions. As I read information and do my research, I am easily scared away by marketing and selling messages. My emotions and fears include:

- Making a decision that will cost me dearly.
- Living in doubt so my self-confidence is low.
- Risky situations that stimulate my emotions and fears.

I can be repelled quickly from an organization's sales message if it doesn't include safety. I admit that I am highly frugal. I'm different from other people who seek value. For example, I'm a person who likes to have maximum coverages for insurance. I like safety systems. With the future seemingly uncertain, I don't rest easily at night.

3. CALM THE MIND

I need to hear calming messages. My anxiety can be high, so I want to be quickly calmed. I warm up to organizations that very quickly show me how my money, health, relationships, and more will be safe with them. I want to be assured and reaffirmed that there is no risk.

Organizations should remember that with me they need to:

- Build my confidence to subdue my fears.
- Know that I'm content when I can find a product or service that helps to fulfill the promise of safety and security.
- Reassure that a proposition is no risk.

Guarantees are important to me because I value safety, above all else. I have to be moved away from the edge. Sometimes I like to see the guarantee early on in the sales message. It reassures me quickly. When I see that there is safety and security for myself and my loved ones, I am far more receptive to marketing messages.

4. POSITION / REPOSITION

I need to see safety in a marketing message. It's essential. There simply can be no risk for me. Anything that can be done that boosts my self-confidence is an extra bonus. I feel more assured with guarantees and testimonials, but I must feel that the positioning of a company is sincere and authentic. When an organization points out how outcomes can be worse if I fail to take action, I will listen.

5. TELL A STORY

I enjoy reading stories that have a happy ending. I want to know that everyone made it home safe and sound. Stories that resonate with me feature people who are cautious about themselves, their money, and their health. I want to be able to participate without feeling like I am going to be burned. I like to see a story that features someone who is a problem solver. I want to know that there is a confident hero in the story, because I will look toward that hero as a role model.

6. INTERPRET

By nature, I am a logical person. That means that any marketing message needs to be persuasive in a way that lays out all of the arguments in a logical sequence. A guarantee is vital for me to see. I never want to feel like I have been burned by overpaying. I must feel comfortable with an offer.

Benefits trump features for me. The benefits must be very clear and flow from the big picture all the way to the details so that I can see multiple parts of the story. The offer must include the safety and security that I require before I make a purchase.

Because I am a bit more pessimistic than optimistic, a marketing message must logically flow so that it aligns with my thought process. I am doubtful of my decisions. But when I find a marketer who helps me solve problems through logical arguments, I am more apt to do business with them.

7. PERMISSION TO ACT

I'm not an individual who feels chills very often. It's probably a slow process to gain my trust and comfort before I give myself permission to act. Ultimately, I have to feel comfortable and secure before making a decision.

I recognize past opportunities that have worked well for me. I'm highly intuitive. For that reason, an organization has to be careful not to repulse me or turn me off by provoking the wrong gut reaction. I need an organization who will work with me to fix any challenges in my perceptions.

I have to be slowly taken to a point where I realize that the marketer's offer is good and smart for me. That means marketers are going to have to work harder to get me to act. But once I trust a marketer, I will be a customer for a very long time, because for me, it's all about safety and security.

CHAPTER 21

PERSONA #9: HIDING MY COMPULSION

1. CORE PERSONA VALUES

I have deep-seated compulsions that need to be regularly fed. Usually I hide them. I'm aware of my compulsions and how destructive they can be to me, both physically and mentally. I yearn for normalcy and continually seek out how to lead a normal life. Secrecy is paramount. Anything I see from marketers must be discreet and private. I want to see support from organizations about what can be done to help what eats away at my core.

There are dozens, probably hundreds, of niche compulsions like mine. Some of those compulsions are painfully apparent and obvious to people, yet some are not. The key for a marketer is to respect my boundaries and barriers. For them to break through requires a certain degree of sensitivity. They must build trust and empathy. It will take time and it will require proof. I'm unlikely to reach out to peers for advice or recommendations, so my social interaction is kept to a minimum. But once an organization has earned my trust, I will be loyal to the core.

2. STIMULATE EMOTION

I fear being found out. Hiding my compulsion is of utmost importance and highly influences my decisions that I make. I see my secret compulsion as a weakness. I was bullied as a child because other kids could see through me at the time when I felt most vulnerable. Childhood experiences have grooved deep memories for me that can never be changed. I fear that no one empathizes with my situation. I fear being ostracized. I fear that the life I have now, as imperfect as it is, could be forever changed in a very bad way with just one misstep. For that reason:

- I fear my compulsions will somehow be exposed for everyone to see.
- I'm always on my guard.
- I continually compensate to cover-up my insecurities.

I fear I will never be normal or even just average. I see myself as an outlier. I prefer to move away from the mainstream. I hope the people around me think of me as normal, but I'm afraid that the perception of me by other people can change in a heartbeat. I see a chink in my armor, and hope that people around me don't perceive my weakness.

3. CALM THE MIND

I seek calm, but my life always seems to be on the edge. That makes it hard for me to ever feel calm. Empathy works. Confidentiality around me works. The promise of a better day is hopeful. But I continue to feel there is a risk of being overpromised a transformation in my life. I've heard that before. It usually doesn't materialize. I want to have pressure eased in my life for just one day. There are a few ways that my mind can be calmed:

- I want to know that I am not alone. This is important to me. But I know that most people hide their secrets so well that it appears that no one else has a compulsion as I do.
- I need to be assured and comforted that an organization can be trusted.
- I want to be assured that there is safety and security by listening to an organization.

I will consider listening to a marketing message if it seems reasonable that I should take a chance with the organization. When I am calmed, I will slowly open up my trust. But I am fragile. Things must go slowly and easily. I may not respond quickly, but I will remember those who treat me with respect.

4. POSITION / REPOSITION

A positioning of empathy works for me. Too often, marketers charge right into their message without taking into account my thoughts and feelings. A marketer must be gentle. A USP that assures me I am not alone with my compulsion will often engage me. I am drawn to safety, and in messaging I want to have the opportunity to see myself as a hero. I need a friend, and that can be communicated through a company's positioning.

5. TELL A STORY

When I hear stories about individuals who share the same issues that I do, an organization can get my instant attention. I want to know that I am not alone, and I want to see how someone was able to prevail over an issue in their lives. I enjoy the human interest, and knowing there are heroes.

Because I am looking for a hero, I can be drawn deeper inside a message. Story is a big hook to me, and a pathway to my attention. I just want to be like other people. I don't see myself as normal, but I do want to see how I might normalize my life. And I like to see how I can live vicariously through others in the story.

Story is an opportunity for me to build trust in an organization. I've been taken advantage of too many times before, so I must see that I am not going to be taken advantage of again. Allow me to step inside the story, and it will be able to pave deeper grooves for a new memory.

6. INTERPRET

I tend to be more emotional than logical. Once I have gained trust and feel that my boundaries will be respected, I will listen. So an organization must interpret features into benefits that are sensitive to my emotions. For me, logic can be best communicated as part of the story. I must be guaranteed safety and confidentiality. A guarantee that is filled with numbers and logic is less persuasive to me than one that is more emotional in tone.

Interpreting price points isn't terribly important. I am so heavily driven by my emotion that a price of a product or service pales in comparison to the benefit that I feel I will receive. That's why for a marketer's logic they must build on benefits upon benefits so that price is not a significant consideration.

7. PERMISSION TO ACT

It can take time to bring me to a tipping point where I come to the conclusion that an organization has my best interests at heart. They'll have to work with me. I have been hurt so many times in my life that I instinctively believe that I'm not going to benefit from an offer. Past memory recall is very strong for me, so a marketer must make a strong, credible point in order to succeed in paving new grooves in my memory. When I feel that, I will know it is time for me to act. That happens after trust has been delivered and I am confident that I will never be betrayed.

CHAPTER 22

PERSONA #10: FIFTY PLUS

1. CORE PERSONA VALUES

I may be over the age of 50, but that's just a number. Being over 50 is a mindset. I have daily reminders that I am aging. There are the daily physical reminders, but as I reach middle age, I recognize that my priorities are changing. My family is growing up. Grandchildren remind me that there is a circle of life. Career aspirations change and retirement looms ahead.

Honestly, I'm tired. There may be other baby boomers who are invigorated, just like the ads I see on TV, but deep down inside, I think it's a front. I wish I could go back in time, as I evoke memories of my youth. I feel that I am on the edge to being beyond the middle age curve. Priorities can change overnight. Suddenly children are young adults and have moved out of the house. My parents are aging, and I see a role reversal, where I am now their caregiver.

Life is often stressful and frightening. My basic survival is front and center. Once upon a time, I imagined enjoyment of later years in my life as I got closer to retirement. But the realities of health, finances, and relationships are a jolting reminder that it's not all happy news. I have come to terms with my reality. I am aging, and there is no turning back the clock.

2. STIMULATE EMOTION

I fear that I won't get to live the happy, carefree life that I see on display in advertising. I fear my health will decline. I fear I haven't saved enough money to retire. I fear and have seen other people experience age discrimination in culture, as well as workplaces that marginalizes older workers.

The circle of life has changed. I'm on a different side of the circle, where it's me, a formidable baby boomer, who is being replaced. Technology changes so rapidly, and it's hard for me to keep up. I didn't get to enjoy using a smartphone, texting, social media, or the Internet until middle age. I've adapted, but I'm weary of keeping up any longer.

I fear my youth and importance as a baby boomer in our culture is coming to an end. I sense the world is passing me by. This point in my life has fears that are becoming more magnified as I see an uncertain future.

3. CALM THE MIND

Despite my fears, as a baby boomer, I can still be calmed. The generation of baby boomers has always been hopeful and optimistic about the future. I just have to be promised that there are resources that will help me. I can be calmed by being reminded that compared to a generation ago, we're healthier and seeing advances only dreamed about by our parents. I see that I have options for a better life.

When I look at marketing messages:

- I want to be reminded that as a baby boomer we are still a reckoning force and relevant.
- I want to see continual breakthroughs, especially in health.
- I want to be assured there are answers for my problems as I enter new phases in my life.
- I want to be taken away, at least temporarily, from the worry of my financial future.

Deep down, I refuse to grow up. I don't see myself as slowing down or giving up. I want to feel like I am at least a decade younger than what I really am. And I want to feel that, as a baby boomer, I am helping to define a new era of people over 50.

4. POSITION / REPOSITION

I am engaged with marketer's product positions when my unique situation and phase of my life is acknowledged. My mind encompasses so many concerns spanning from health and wealth to lifestyle, along with being an empty nester and caring for a parent. I have multitudes of concerns.

I want to see positioning that recognizes and identifies my relative age, and then helps to offer me a place that defines my life in a new and better way. A few of those ideas include:

- Mentally transforming me to a place where I can feel younger, but don't dwell on reminding me of my youth from decades ago.
- An organization that can help me with the burdens of life today

Make no mistake: I have fond memories of the 1960s and 70s. I get nostalgic sometimes. Those were turbulent times in American history; not unlike what we experience today. I've been there, and I've done that. But I still want to be taken to a place of happy memories. I like a bit of nostalgia because it's fun to be taken back to a time that I wish I could relive again.

5. TELL A STORY

I love stories. I want to hear about people like myself. I've gone through unique experiences during my lifetime, especially from the decades of the 1960s and 70s. Those were the golden years for baby boomers. I like to hear stories about other people my age and solutions to health concerns, financial pressures, and other concerns that people over the age of 50 can relate to.

I have many concerns weighing on my mind. There are the physical reminders of aging. My children are now young adults, and I worry about how they are going to make it in today's world. But I'm also concerned about aging parents. It's helpful to know how others dealing with similar circumstances are dealing with these pressures.

I am acutely aware that there is no turning back the clock. No story can change that. But I have deeply ingrained memories that make me smile. When I hear a story or read a story from a marketer, it must be relevant to the era in time that I look back on. I want to be led to thinking that there could be a brighter future than what I envision.

6. INTERPRET

There is so much noise and a bombardment of information and choices that the interpretation of information must go to my heart. I'm over the age of 50, and at a different point in my life. It's a place I've never known or experienced before. I need complex information explained to me.

Logical arguments from my peers are more credible to me. I'm also beginning to listen to the logical arguments of generations older than me. As baby boomers, we didn't always trust those who are older than us. We were the ones, after all, who were leading a new charge in the culture of the world. But now that I am aging, I appreciate and respect what people who are younger than me are saying about those who are older. The millennial generation, represented by my children, is beginning to become a stronger influence in my life.

The changing economy has been difficult for me. As technology rapidly changes around me, I'm not always as quick to adapt it. I look to younger people who can help me, so I want to hear from an organization who understands that dynamic.

I'm also entering a point in my life where I am more price sensitive than I used to be. Economic challenges in recent years have stripped away money. I feel I've lost time in saving for retirement. My confidence to spend money isn't as high as it once was. I must see a logical argument that will show endurance of product. I need to know it will last long or that it will significantly improve my life.

Guarantees are important to me. I've seen too many points of disruption in recent years and I'm worried that things will change greatly in the future.

7. PERMISSION TO ACT

I have had so many different life experiences that I'm weary. When I'm taken to a place about something in my sub conscious mind, I realize some of the things that I should be doing now. I know that I should be saving for my financial future. I know that I should be eating healthy food and exercising to doing better things for my health. There are so many complex issues as a person ages. I'd like to hide those thoughts and think that those realities don't exist. So a marketer needs to bring it forward in my mind and take me to a place where I have to give myself permission to act.

Enable me to feel youthful again and invoke a pleasant past memory. Show me how that past and pleasant memory in my life will benefit me now. I have many perceptions that have been built over many years of my life. Some of those must be overcome. When that happens, I will feel chills. Then I can conclude on my own that "this is good, this is smart, and I will give myself permission to act."

CHAPTER 23

PERSONA #11: BUSINESS 8 TO 5

1. CORE PERSONA VALUES

By day, I take on a different persona from that of my personal life. It's all about business. I work in an office. I have people around me all day long. I have a boss and co-workers. It's not necessarily how I would choose to live my time Monday through Friday from 8 to 5, but it's what I do to make a living.

Sometimes I am tasked with making decisions that involve purchasing products for my company. I'm not always the final person to make the decision, but I will have input on it. The money is not my own. And my job can be on the line for how I spend the company's money. So I need to make smart decisions that will help improve the profitability of my organization.

Deep down, I am most concerned about my job security. So for that reason, I am very protective and thoughtful when it comes to spending the company's money.

2. STIMULATE EMOTION

I feel pretty good about my job security, but there is always a fear of screwing up. It might not result in me being fired, but it can show up on a job review in the future. And can have negative lasting results for my ability to be promoted in the future.

197

In instances where I am unhappy with a current vendor, my emotion can be stimulated if I see a better approach that will improve my company's bottom line.

My emotion is also stimulated any time there is a possible threat to either my job security or how I will be viewed in the office. I'm very sensitive to any outcome concerning change.

3. CALM THE MIND

I am at my calmest when I'm able to just do my job without any interference. There is safety in continuing to use the same vendor, rather than finding a new vendor because it's a known entity. Changing vendors for anything in my company is risky for me. So I'm at my calmest when things are the status quo.

If a prospective vendor approaches me, I must be quickly reassured that a possible change could result in making me look good to my bosses. There needs to be proof that a change in relationship could benefit me. Still, I will proceed with caution even if I see an upside.

4. POSITION / REPOSITION

I need to know that a prospective vendor can fulfill my company's requirements. In situations where I am happy with the current vendor, I need to understand how a new vendor is unique. In situations where I am not satisfied with the current vendor, I need to understand how a new vendor will be different and better than the status quo. Either way, I must see how a company's product or service is decidedly different from what I'm currently doing now before I will give them the time of day.

5. TELL A STORY

I don't hear stories very often in business-to-business communications. Yes, I hear testimonials. But stories impact me more. It's tough to break through to score my business. But a story could serve to be influential in how I view and respond to a prospective change from a company where I already do business. I want to hear how another company was able to become more profitable. I realize that most companies don't want to share their results, so I understand that a story can be difficult for a B2B marketer to share. But I would even be interested in listening to a story about how a company was easy to work with and provided great service.

6. INTERPRET

It's important that I see features and benefits side-by-side. I need to be able to see those comparisons so that I can make an objective decision. If something goes wrong in a new business relationship, I will want to point at evidence that gets me off the hook. I can't have all eyes and the blame on me if a decision goes badly.

I want to see a strong guarantee. I need to have promised features put in writing. I will need to read your agreement and have any contracts approved.

Pricing is important to understand. I am most annoyed when I am promised one price but then delivered another. When I'm comparison shopping, one thing that really irritates me is how companies provide quotes that are confusing and inconsistent with how others price their products or services. Transparency in pricing is important.

7. PERMISSION TO ACT

It takes a quite a bit to move me to the tipping point of making a decision to respond. I'll need to proceed one step at a time. It probably means that I'm going to initially ask the vendor for some basic information so that I can start research. That's pretty easy. But I don't want to feel like I'm opening myself up to being hounded by a salesperson.

If a company has built my trust in them, I'm more apt to give myself permission to act, even if it's just to inquire. But I may need to have several conversations that lead to a purchase decision. It may be a process. But ultimately what will take me to a point to give myself the permission to either endorse, support, or outright make a purchase decision will be my confidence that they can deliver and that there will be no surprises.

CHAPTER 24

PERSONA #12: DID I MATTER?

1. CORE PERSONA VALUES

I have found my purpose in life, and I want to leave a legacy that fulfills that purpose. I continually work toward fulfilling my mission while I'm alive. I would like to see my legacy remembered now, while I can see how my money is put to good use, as well as after I'm gone.

I make decisions about what organizations I contribute to based on the alignment of their passion and purpose with my own. I'm not an overly wealthy individual, but I have financial resources that enable me to leave a legacy.

I want my family to enjoy money that I have worked to earn, but I also want to share it beyond my family. I would like something that furthers a part of my life story. It would be affirming to know that my money is being used now and then after I'm gone for something positive. I feel an enormous sense of pride and goodwill, knowing that my money is being used for a good cause.

2. STIMULATE EMOTION

I fear that the good things I have done in my life won't be completely recognized. I fear being forgotten after I am gone, and that my relevance will slowly dissipate. I fear that my skills will be less important. I want the skills that I have accumulated over my lifetime to be recognized and appreciated. I fear:

- My contributions to humanity will leave me largely unimportant in the world.
- My life is incomplete.
- Being forgotten by people important to me in my life now and in future generations.

After spending so much of my life in other endeavors, I've begun to realize that I don't want to be seen as irrelevant. As I reach the point of end-of-life planning, I can reduce my fears with generosity. And I don't want to be seen as someone who accumulated wealth and didn't share it. By giving, I can moderate my fear of being perceived as greedy.

3. CALM THE MIND

I want to feel that I can live on forever. That calms me. I understand there are varying degrees of how my legacy can be left. I realize that it is simple for some people. I deeply desire assurances that my inner circle of family and friends will remember me in a positive light. I know there are others who want to make a difference on a more global scale, often with complete strangers and anonymously. I want assurance that:

- My life is adding value to our world and culture.
- My life has been important.
- I will be remembered long after I am gone.

I am a multifaceted individual. I'm a person who is righteous in my belief. I'm careful with my money and thoughtful about cultivating my brand. But I am afraid that my legacy will be lost, so I need to have reason to see that my personal identity will be viewed as important.

4. POSITION / REPOSITION

I am open to the positioning statement of an organization that offers to show me how my money will be used well. I'm also open to making plans now for the future. Just remember, though: I'm not dead yet! So I am sensitive to those who suggest otherwise.

I continue to weigh many options in my life. I look at a multitude of organizations so that I know there is competition for my dollars. But I want to see that I will be honored for years to come. I want to see that the cause or the product I'm being offered promises to fill an emptiness for the rest of my life.

5. TELL A STORY

I enjoy hearing stories about people whose lives have been remembered in a favorable light. This helps to illustrate how others have seen a pathway to fulfilling their life's mission, and how I might be remembered. When I see how someone else's purpose has been enhanced, I go along with the story. It helps me find what I have been searching for my entire life.

I enjoy seeing how others have had emptiness in their heart and mind fulfilled. Uplifting stories take me to a place where I am at peace. It helps me understand that my life really has had purpose and that my values have been fulfilled while I am still alive.

I hate to admit it, but my ego plays a large role in my decisions. Maybe that means I'm a bit insecure, too, but I'm obsessed with knowing that my life has mattered. And stories help affirm me of that possibility for me in the future.

6. INTERPRET

I'm a logical person. I want to understand step-by-step how my money is used today, and how I am going to be remembered. I like to see organizations recognize that they understand my life's purpose. I want to see that my dreams and goals are put into action.

I want to understand how I am going to be remembered. And since I don't always know myself how I want to be remembered, it's helpful to be given illustrations of how that might look. I want to be convinced that there will be long-lasting goodwill created because of the choices that I make now.

This is a significant emotional decision for me. I understand that there can be no guarantee that I will be remembered forever, but I want assurances that steps will be taken so that I will be remembered for a long time to come.

7. PERMISSION TO ACT

Before I will give myself permission to contribute to a cause where I can be remembered, I need to be awakened with overwhelming emotion. When that happens, I will feel goosebumps and chills. A tipping point can be if I feel that I will be taken from obscurity to fame.

When pleasant memories of the past can be invoked, it helps to symbolize who I was in my lifetime, and demonstrate that whatever an organization offers will provide a form of legacy for me. I want to know that whatever my choices, this is going to be good and smart for me, and good and smart for future generations.

ABOUT THE AUTHOR

Gary Hennerberg is a veteran marketing professional, equally accomplished in the dual roles of copywriter/creative director and analytic consultant. He has created and overseen hundreds of marketing campaigns that have reached tens of millions of households and businesses around the world. He is in demand as a consultant, speaker, trainer and author.

Hennerberg has reinvented his skills multiple times in his career. As a former marketing and product manager, agency executive, and now an in-demand consultant, creative director, and trainer, he has successfully transferred traditional offline marketing principles to online media. He has been a marketing professional since 1978 and an independent marketing consultant and copywriter since 1992.

As a marketing turnaround consultant, he searches for new and incremental sales dollars for marketing organizations. With experience in cross-channel marketing, Hennerberg recommends the most effective and cost-efficient blend to generate sales. He is sought-after for his analysis skills and creative integration of websites, email, direct mail, content marketing, search marketing, retargeting and more.

When he has followed the seven pathways in the mind, as detailed in *Crack the Customer Mind Code*, his work has resulted in sales increases of 15%, 35%, and even as high as 60%.

Hennerberg is the author of *Direct Marketing Quantified: The Knowledge is in the Numbers*, and *Urges*, a memoir about his childhood growing up with hair pulling disorder.

He has been a long-time writer for *Target Marketing Magazine* and has authored of dozens of articles on marketing best practices, and has spoken at numerous conferences and events.

Read more about Gary Hennerberg at CustomerMindCode.com.

END NOTES

1 Q, B. (2010, July 11). 'Invisible Gorilla' Test Shows How Little We Notice. Retrieved from http://www.livescience.com/6727-invisible-gorilla-test-shows-notice.html

2 A comparison of the cell phone driver and the drunk driver. Retrieved from http://www.ncbi.nlm.nih.gov/pubmed/16884056

3 Higher Media Multi-Tasking Activity Is Associated with Smaller Gray-Matter Density in the Anterior Cingulate Cortex. Retrieved from http://journals.plos.org/plosone/article?id=10.1371/journal.pone.0106698

4 BRAIN Initiative. (n.d.). Retrieved from https://www.whitehouse.gov/share/brain-initiative

5 Mental disorders affect one in four people. (n.d.). Retrieved from http://www.who.int/whr/2001/media_centre/press_release/en/

6 Brainstormers: Obama's big research push kicks off with a meeting of the minds. (n.d.). Retrieved from http://www.washingtonpost.com/national/health-science/obama-research-initiative-seeks-to-create-new-tools-to-understand-the-human-brain/2015/01/02/dce17f02-7bb8-11e4-9a27-6fdbc612bff8_story.html

7 How social media is reshaping news. (2014, September 24). Retrieved from http://www.pewresearch.org/fact-tank/2014/09/24/how-social-media-is-reshaping-news/

8 How great leaders inspire action. (n.d.). Retrieved from http://www.ted.com/talks/simon_sinek_how_great_leaders_inspire_action

9 The 5 Big Mistakes That Led to Ron Johnson's Ouster at JC Penney | TIME.com. (n.d.). Retrieved from http://business.time.com/2013/04/09/the-5-big-mistakes-that-led-to-ron-johnsons-ouster-at-jc-penney/

10 Another Big Five for Personality. (n.d.). Retrieved from https://www.psychologytoday.com/blog/theory-knowledge/201204/another-big-five-personality

11 Attention Span Statistics. (n.d.). Retrieved from http://www.statisticbrain.com/attention-span-statistics/

12 Report: 56% of Social Media Users Suffer From FOMO. (n.d.). Retrieved from http://mashable.com/2013/07/09/fear-of-missing-out/

13 How Sweet Talk Emotionally Engages The Brain. (n.d.). Retrieved from http://psychcentral.com/news/2014/06/28/how-sweet-talk-emotionally-engages-the-brain/71848.html

14 Pavlov's Dogs | Simply Psychology. (n.d.). Retrieved from http://www.simplypsychology.org/pavlov.html

15 Sylwester, R. (1995). A celebration of neurons: An educator's guide to the human brain. Alexandria, Va.: Association for Supervision and Curriculum Development.

16 Written all over your face: Humans express four basic emotions rather than six, says new study. (n.d.). Retrieved from http://www.gla.ac.uk/news/headline_306019_en.html

17 Empathy, Neurochemistry, and the Dramatic Arc. (n.d.). Retrieved from https://www.youtube.com/watch?v=dSyyAcrsnT4&feature=youtu.be

18 The Emotions of Highly Viral Content –. (2013, July 9). Retrieved from http://frac.tl/viral-emotions-study/

19 What Makes Online Content Viral? (n.d.). Retrieved from http://journals.ama.org/doi/abs/10.1509/jmr.10.0353

20 Goethe, J. (1906). Physiological colours, from Goethe's "Outline of a theory of colours".

21 (n.d.). Retrieved from http://www.sciencedaily.com/releases/2014/04/140408112210.htm

22 Belluck, P. (2009, February 5). Reinvent Wheel? Blue Room. Defusing a Bomb? Red Room. Retrieved from http://www.nytimes.com/2009/02/06/science/06color.html?_r=2&

23 Stop On Red! The Effects of Color May Lie Deep in Evolution.... (n.d.). Retrieved from http://www.psychologicalscience.org/index.php/news/

releases/stop-on-red-a-monkey-study-suggests-that-the-effects-of-color-lie-deep-in-evolution.html

24 Brand Equity Models and Measurement | Marketing Research Association. (n.d.). Retrieved from http://www.marketingresearch.org/issues-policies/best-practice/brand-equity-models-and-measurement

25 Reeves, R. (1961). Reality in advertising. New York: Knopf.

26 Smartphone Users Play Games to Relieve Stress - eMarketer. (n.d.). Retrieved from http://www.emarketer.com/Article/Smartphone-Users-Play-Games-Relieve-Stress/1010523

27 High Definition: The 'Gamification' of the Office Approaches. (n.d.). Retrieved from http://www.wsj.com/news/articles/SB10001424052702303819704579316721461148950?mod=WSJ_hps_MIDDLE_Video_Top

28 Green, P. (2012, July 11). He Takes Stuff Seriously. Retrieved from http://www.nytimes.com/2012/07/12/garden/at-home-with-joshua-glenn-of-the-significant-objects-project.html?pagewanted=all&_r=0) NOTE: link requires a log-in

29 (n.d.). Retrieved from http://online.liebertpub.com/doi/pdf/10.1089/brain.2013.0166

30 Harris, R. (2003). Pompeii: A novel. New York: Random House.

31 The Irresistible Power of Storytelling as a Strategic Business Tool. (n.d.). Retrieved from https://hbr.org/2014/03/the-irresistible-power-of-storytelling-as-a-strategic-business-tool/

32 Freytag's Pyramid. (n.d.). Retrieved from https://web.cn.edu/kwheeler/freytag.html

33 Golin/Harris Trust Survey Finds 69 Percent of Americans Say 'I Just Don't Know Whom to Trust Anymore' (n.d.). Retrieved from http://www.prnewswire.com/news-releases/golinharris-trust-survey-finds-69-percent-of-americans-say-i-just-dont-know-whom-to-trust-anymore-76165032.html

34 Harvard Business School. (n.d.). Retrieved from http://hbswk.hbs.edu/item/7651.html?sf34775801=1

35 American Writers & Artists Inc., 245 NE 4th Ave., Ste 102, Delray Beach, FL 33483, (561) 278-5557 or (866) 879-2924, http://www.awaionline. com/

36 Illiteracy Statistics. (n.d.). Retrieved from http://www.statisticbrain.com/ number-of-american-adults-who-cant-read/

37 Zhao, E. (n.d.). American High School Students Are Reading Books At 5th-Grade-Appropriate Levels: Report. Retrieved from http://www. huffingtonpost.com/2012/03/22/top-reading_n_1373680.html

38 (n.d.). Retrieved from http://www.theguardian.com/world/ interactive/2013/feb/12/state-of-the-union-reading-level

39 Cialdini, R. (1984). Influence: How and why people agree to things. New York: Morrow. http://www.influenceatwork.com/

40 Why digital natives prefer reading in print. Yes, you read that right. (n.d.) from http://www.washingtonpost.com/local/why-digital-natives-prefer-reading-in-print-yes-you-read-that-right/2015/02/22/8596ca86-b871-11e4-9423-f3d0a1ec335c_story.html

41 Taking reading comprehension exams on screen or on paper? A metacognitive analysis of learning texts under time pressure. (n.d.). Retrieved from http://www.academia.edu/1245333/Taking_reading_comprehension_exams_on_screen_or_on_paper_A_metacognitive_analysis_of_learning_texts_under_time_pressure

42 The Reading Brain in the Digital Age: The Science of Paper versus Screens. (n.d.). Retrieved from http://www.scientificamerican.com/article/reading-paper-screens/

CUSTOMERMINDCODE.COM RESOURCES

Gary Hennerberg is available for speaking, in-house training, marketing consulting and creative services.

Refer to CustomerMindCode.com for content updates and new training programs as they become available.

Printed in the USA
CPSIA information can be obtained
at www.ICGtesting.com
JSHW022325140824
68134JS00019B/1305

9 781630 476984